Sue Laflin-Barker's Start Ancient Wargaming with DBA 3.0

Edited by John Curry

There are over sixty books currently edited or written by John Curry as part of the History of Wargaming Project. These include:

See The History of Wargaming Project at *www.wargaming.co* for other publications.

ISBN 978-1-326-07501-9

Cover illustration: A Palmyran army faces up to the Romans.

Contents

Chapter Six: A Selection of Army Lists   119

ACKNOWLEDGEMENTS

I owe special thanks to my husband Phil Barker for his support and encouragement during the writing of this book and also for his permission to include the *DBA* rules in this book. All the *DBA* revising committee spread over three continents, who have worked so hard over the last few years have also indirectly contributed to this book and I wish to express my thanks. Especial mention must be made to the smaller group who have contributed directly to the development of this book. They are John S. Brown, Joe Collins, Pete Duckworth, Chris Hanley, Bill MacGillivray, Keith McNelly, Doug Melville, Thomas J. Thomas and especially Bob Beattie. I thank them all. Finally I should also acknowledge my partners in WRG Ltd who have given permission to include the title *De Bellis Antiquitatis* which has now been trademarked in the UK.

Sue Laflin-Barker. September 2014.

Foreword

DBA is amongst that rare breed of wargaming rules; it has been enduring and popular for over twenty five years. Written by a team effort of Phil Barker, Sue Laflin-Barker and Richard Bodley Scott, it was a radical shift from the wargames that had gone before. The interesting story of the *DBA* rules was included in the book *DBA 2.2 Simple Ancient and Medieval Wargaming Rules* (also published by the *History of Wargaming Project*). DBA has developed from the first edition of the rules presented at the *Conference of Wargamers* and the *Society of Ancients Conference* in 1989 and now, in 2014, the rules are version 3.0.

When the WRG Ancient Rules were first published in 1969, they were soon very popular amongst the tiny number of wargamers in the world. As the hobby of wargaming expanded, there were new players who were keen to start, but who needed a guide to help them get started in ancient wargaming. There were calls for a book about ancient wargaming to accompany the WRG rules. In 1975, Phil Barker answered this call and wrote *The Airfix Guide to Ancient Wargaming*; this so called 'The Purple Primer' provided such a guide and was sought after second hand long after it was out of print.

The aim of this new book by Sue Laflin-Barker is to provide a new 'Purple Primer' for those starting the hobby of ancient and medieval wargaming with the *DBA* rules. It covers a range of topics from choosing and assembling an army, to a discussion of the rules and sample army lists with explanations. This guide has been written for the current version of the *DBA* rules, version 3.0 and it is hoped this book will be of equal utility as its predecessor, The original 'Purple Primer'.

John Curry
Editor of the History of Wargaming Project
December 2014

Biographical Notes on Sue Laflin-Barker

Sue was born in November 1940 in the middle of an air raid and grew up in the depths of rural England as a child. She was fortunate enough to win a scholarship to the local Grammar School, in the days where fine education was not universally available. She found she had some academic ability and she took the opportunity to learn Latin and Greek and well as Mathematics, and Science. This allowed her to read Mathematics at London University and later, to work in the Space Research Department of the well-known academic institution, UCL. She finished her lecturing career as a Lecturer in Computer Science at the prestigious University of Birmingham (England, not USA).

She became interested in wargaming after her marriage to Phil Barker in 1969. She then joined the Society of Ancients and served in their Committee and ran their Wargames Championship for several years.

At the same time she helped Phil Barker with WRG, such as by attending conventions and running trade stands. Over the years she travelled widely with him to wargames meeting all over the world. She was also co-author with Phil of the tremendously popular HOTT and *DBA* rules.

She took the opportunity to retire from lecturing in 2000, leaving more time for other interests. This has included authoring several books on her family history. She is still very active in wargaming and joined the new WRG Ltd Company as a Director and Chairman.

Start Ancient Wargaming is her first solo authorship of a wargames book.

Chapter One: Introduction.

This book contains instructions for creating and painting armies, creating the terrain for battlefields, a bound-by-bound account of a game, a copy of the rules for *De Bellis Antiquitatis* (*DBA*) version 3.0 and a selection of army lists for the whole world and the whole period from 3000BC to 1500AD, organised into pairs of historically matched opponents.

This is a personal account of the things learned when one wargamer's wife (myself) decided take up the hobby. I have written this book in the hope that other newcomers to the hobby will benefit from my experiences. I have now been active as a wargamer for over forty years and have learnt a great deal during that time – however I make no claim for completeness in what follows. There are other ways of doing things and some of you may prefer them. The ones described here worked for me.

To some outside the hobby, the term "war-games" appears to be a contradiction. War is not a game: it is deadly serious and people get killed or maimed. No-one disputes this, but some of my acquaintances (I won't call them friends) disapprove of the hobby (probably because it sounds like actual warfare) and especially when enjoyed by me, a woman. They are too busy disapproving to listen and so I cannot explain I have no intention of taking part in a game which makes fun of the courage and sacrifice of the members of the armed forces – in fact I doubt whether such games actually exist. Instead the type of wargaming I enjoy takes one aspect of actual warfare - namely the tactical deployment of troops on a battlefield - and develops this into various games using model soldiers on the model of a battlefield. Chess is one example of such a game; *DBA* is another.

Wargaming is not the only example of a single aspect of war becoming divorced from it and developing into a separate activity. Other examples are Olympic sports such as wrestling, javelin-throwing, boxing, fencing and shooting. They have now become accepted as sports in their own right and the earlier connection with warfare has been forgotten. The athletes who excel at these sports are rightly respected for their skill and no-one fears that they will use this expertise to wage war against their neighbours.

In wargaming, we have games which were originally used to train leaders in the tactics of moving troops on a battlefield. Chess is one example of such a game, but it has become stylised over the centuries.

The battlefield has become a checkerboard of black and white squares. The troops are represented by single models. The different abilities of the troops survive only as the different moves of the various pieces. Even so some things remain such as the challenge of pitting your wits against an opponent, followed by the thrill of victory or the disappointment of defeat. The same is true of the Viking game "Hnefltafl".

Wargames such as DBA may be thought of as a more colourful form of chess. The playing pieces (called "elements") are cardboard bases with a number of model soldiers painted and stuck to them and each one represents a unit of troops. The playing area is small and is laid out to represent an area of country-side to be used as the battlefield. Unlike chess, the rules also allow the possibility of multi-player games with a group of players on each side and this provides companionship. So does belonging to a wargames club.

There are many sets of rules for wargaming and this book describes one set for ancient wargaming. *De Bellis Antiquitatis* (which means "concerning ancient warfare" and is usually shortened to *DBA*) simulates warfare in the "pre-gunpowder period". That is from the earliest period for which we have information (about 3000 BC) up to the period when the introduction of gunpowder started to have a major impact on warfare (around 1500 AD).

Example of a medieval wargame

In DBA the playing area is small (2 or 3 feet square depending on the scale of the figures used) and is laid out to represent a battlefield. Each player has 12 elements making up the entire army. The size of base and the number of figures tell you what type of troops they are and the models themselves show how the troops are equipped. The deployment area from which each army starts is defined by the rules, but after that, the elements may move in any direction although the maximum distance they may move is defined by their type. For example light horse can move much further than heavy infantry. Most sets of rules for table-top gaming work in a similar way.

Different people enjoy different parts of the hobby. Some enjoy making things – collecting and painting the troops and building the model terrain. Others enjoy the experimental approach to history and archaeology, using the rules to test their theories and seeking out information about the armies and the civilisations which created them. (Remember you can never prove that a theory is true but rules like DBA are very good at showing the flaws in theories which are not correct.) Others merely enjoy playing the game, pitting their wits against all comers in the hope of becoming the champion of their club.

Table-top games are not the only type of wargame around. If you type "Wargames" into a search engine such as Google, you will get a wide choice of sites, only a few of which relate to table-top gaming.

Photograph from a 1978 Viking re-enactment

First, we have the various re-enactment societies whose members attempt to recreate warfare during various historical periods. In the United Kingdom we find the Ermine Street Guard (for the Roman period), various Dark Age and Viking groups (the picture shows the *Norse Film and Pageant Society* giving a demonstration at *Northern Militaire* in 1978), medieval tournaments as well as warfare, and a number of groups recreating the English Civil war and the Napoleonic wars. In America you will find the Society for Creative Anachronism (medieval fantasy) and a number of groups re-enacting the American Civil war. Such societies are not directly connected with the wargames discussed here, but their research into the costumes and relative effectiveness of the different armour and weapons has been used to develop these rules.

Finally there are the many board-games and computer games. Mostly these relate to one particular battle or war and are difficult to extend to the more general case. This usually means that if you want to move on to another scenario you will need to purchase another game.

Chapter Two: Choosing and Preparing Your Armies

2.1 Historical Introduction

When you set out to play *DBA* or any other similar wargame, the first thing you need is an army or a pair of armies. An experienced wargamer is likely to have figures from which armies can be built up, but a complete newcomer will start from nothing. This was my position when I entered wargaming and this chapter contains a personal account of how I started and an example of how I would set out to produce a pair of armies. It is not the only way to do things and experienced gamers may have different ideas, but it is one way to produce the necessary armies.

When I started in the early 1970s, the easiest figures to obtain were 20 or 25mm metal figures. My husband Phil suggested I choose the army of Queen Zenobia of Palmyra and gave me some of his figures to get started. These were fully-armoured cataphracts and I found a suitable figure for Zenobia herself.

Then I needed some archers and I bought two identical units. I started playing – this was the third edition of the original WRG ancient rules involving the "reaction test". At intervals throughout the game, some or all of the units had to take a "reaction test" which meant that the player threw three dice and added in the relevant factors. If the resulting score was comfortably in the middle of the range, the unit continued to obey its orders. However, three sixes often meant they charged the nearest enemy regardless of the likely outcome, while three ones might mean that they fled off the battlefield.

In one of my early games, one of these archer units had high dice for its reaction, ignoring its bows and instead charging into the enemy. The other had low dice, and retreated off the battlefield. This happened in several games and by coincidence it was always the same unit that charged and the other who fled. I soon found myself expecting them to behave in this way. I added a hunting cheetah to Zenobia's base to fetch the cowards back and their dice improved slightly.

Now this has to be an illusion – they are metal figures and they cannot really acquire characters. However I have to admit they did appear to do so and many other wargamers have found the same. I decided this must be a figment of my imagination – remembering the cases when the dice did produce the expected results and forgetting the occasions when they did not.

But worse was to come. I called the cowards "lamp-androi" being a translation of "Flashman's lot" (If you haven't yet met the *Flashman* novels by George MacDonald Fraser then you have a treat in store) and gave them an officer with a Greek lamda on his shield. When I came to sell them, the new owner thought this meant they were super-brave Spartans – that was what he expected. However in spite of his expectations, their first reaction dice was three ones and they left the table without firing a shot. I am told they continued to behave in the same way. I cannot explain this.

My next army was Ancient Britons with Queen Cartimandua in command. For these I bought, painted and converted Airfix plastic figures. As the years rolled by, I continued to buy additional figures – including metal ones as they became available – and I now have my original Cartinadua with a new 25mm metal chariot and charioteer. Since the Brigantes are known to have been a collection of tribal groups, I organised them into such groups using colours to denote them. They seemed to fight well with the warband as the main attack force supported by chariots, light horse and slingers.

Cartimandua in her chariot

My Cartimandua, shown in the picture, was the woman from the Airfix wagon train with a Battersea shield attached – fat and forty rather than the glamorous 'dolly-bird' which so many manufacturers produced for Cartimandua. However, I reasoned that if she was already Queen of the Brigantes when Claudius invaded Britain in 43 AD then by the middle of the first century she must have been around forty years old and this figure seemed to me to be correct. I still have these figures although I do not use them very much these days.

Soon after this, the 15mm ranges started to appear and I bought armies in this scale as being cheaper to buy and easier to store and carry around. When DBM first appeared I collected and painted a large 15mm Ancient British army, only to find that I always had to send a large contingent on a flank march because the deployment area on the table was not large enough to cram them all in (This changed in the next edition). Once again the dice started "thinking for themselves" – there is a one in six chance of a flank march arriving but my sub-general never arrived on the table and I came to expect him to behave in this way.

If I were starting again now, I would choose DBA and I would choose pairs of historical opponents so that the battle would be historically accurate as well as fun. Once you start to look into the possibilities, you will find a very large range of figures available. Each army consists of twelve "elements" made of rectangular cardboard bases with suitable models stuck onto them. Elephants, chariots and artillery have one model per base while infantry and cavalry have several figures per base. The number of figures varies depending on the type of troops.

2.2 Types of Figures.

It is possible to buy cardboard armies online. Type "paper armies" into an Internet search engine such as Google and you will find a number of sites offering such armies. They provide cardboard bases of the correct size for *DBA* printed with a view from above of a suitable element. Another similar site is "Junior General" which allows you to download both troops and terrain. They can be used to try out the rules. So can plain cardboard bases with the troop type written on them. Personally, I would not wish to use them because none of these have the same attraction as solid figures, even crudely painted ones.

You may go on to eBay and buy a pair of ready painted armies, in which case you can skip the rest of this chapter. This is the quickest option, but probably one of the more expensive. Or you may pick up an army in a "bring and buy" sale at a local wargames show. Most wargamers prefer to buy the unpainted figures and then paint them in the colours of their own choosing. Some professional painters offer a painting service and this is a suitable option for those who can afford it.

The most popular scale is 15mm and many manufacturers (including Essex, Donnington, Bacchus, Museum Miniatures, and Xyston) offer boxes containing a complete metal *DBA* army in this scale. Some include pictures on their website so that you can see what you are ordering – others merely list the contents of the pack. If you wish to choose this route, you should go online and explore what is available.

Some of you may prefer smaller figures and these can be found in all scales from 15mm down to 2mm. Irregular Miniatures is but one of the suppliers who have a very wide range of figures and scales. The smaller scales can be mounted on the same bases as the 15mm figures and the *DBA* rules describe the number of figures or models to mount in each element.

The 25mm figures are still available, but some manufacturers have moved to 28mm and there are some very attractive figures available in both metal and hard plastic in this scale. Type "28 mm figures" into a search engine and you will find a selection of websites describing these. My particular favourites are Wargames Foundry, Gripping Beast and Perry Miniatures. However I do find I have to be very careful when shopping online lest I get carried away by the large selection on offer and end up with a huge bill to pay!

Plastic figures are usually made in the 1/72 scale. This scale is approximately 20mm (meaning that a 6ft infantry man will stand 20mm high) - in between the two standard scales for *DBA* (15mm or 25mm) so they are either large 15mm figures or small 25mm figures. If you are able to mount your armies on 15mm bases, you will find a much larger selection of opponents and this is an advantage when you start to visit clubs or enter competitions. However, if the models will not fit onto these bases, then they will need to be treated as a small 25mm army. The quality varies immensely – some are very crude and I would not recommend them while others are beautifully designed with good detail and varied poses. You will need to use *www.plasticsoldierreview.com* or a similar website to examine the figures before deciding which to choose. Such a site will contain pictures and also tell you how many figures are included in each box.

2.3 Scales in *DBA*.

DBA has two standard scales – the "larger scale" which is intended for 25mm or larger figures and has a base width ("BW") of 60mm and the "smaller scale" which is intended for 15mm or smaller figures and has a base width of 40mm. The choice of BW is very important because everything else depends on it – the battlefield is a square with each side approximately 15BW and the movement distances and shooting ranges are defined in terms of BW. It is essential that both armies in any game have the SAME choice of BW. If you choose to use a standard BW then you can go to a club or convention anywhere in the world and find other players with compatible armies. This is a big advantage and you should think very carefully before throwing it away.

However if you decide that you will NEVER want to play outside your own small group, then there is no reason why you cannot choose a non-standard definition of BW for your own group. If you have large figures which are too difficult to fit on the standard BW of 60mm, then you could decide to choose a BW of 80mm. This would mean scaling everything else up to match but having done so your own private club could happily play *DBA* among yourselves. The other possibility in this case is to keep the standard BW and mount fewer figures on the base.

At the other extreme, if you are VERY short of space (possibly because you and your friends are living in a student hall of residence) you might decide to go for a mini*DBA* with 6mm or even 2mm figures, and BW of 20mm instead of the standard 40mm for the smaller scale. This would mean you could happily play on a single carpet tile for your battlefield with the terrain scaled down to match. So long as you scale EVERYTHING, you will still be playing the same game. Base depths in the *DBA* rules are specified in mm and you will need to scale them to match – if your chosen BW is half that of the standard 40mm then all base depths will also need to be halved.

2.4 Choosing your Armies.

As an example, I decided to produce the two armies for **Conflict No: 16 Romans versus Germans** described in Chapter Six. I went to the website *www.plasticsoldierreview.com* to look for suitable armies. For many of these armies, the website lists the contents of the boxes and also includes photographs of the figures. By comparing the figures needed for the armies and the contents of the boxes, I decided I could model the following two armies who might have met in the hills or forests of northern Europe around 100BC. Historically the Romans did not venture far enough into Germany to meet the Cherusci until later in the period, after the Roman armies had been reorganised by Augustus (II/56) in 25BC, but there is no reason to suppose that the Cherusci army changed during this period and these armies allow us to imagine what would have happened if they had met.

The Roman Army.

    1 general in an element of Legionaries (4Bd)
    1 element of LH with javelins.
    7 elements of Legionaries (4 Blades to each element).
    2 elements of Skirmishers (2 psiloi).
    1 element of cavalry

So this requires 32 Roman legionary figures including at least one officer (for the general) accompanied by an eagle-bearer and musician figure. Some of the other figures could also be officers. Also the army will need 4 suitable figures for skirmishers (some from the German box), The mounted figure intended as a Roman general can be used for the cavalry officer and 4 more mounted figures will be needed (from the Cavalry box).

The Early German (Cherusci) Army.

    1 general with an element of 3 Cavalry.
    9 elements of Warband (3 to each element).
    2 elements of Skirmishers (2 psiloi) armed with javelins.

This will need 3 mounted figures, 27 warband figures assuming 3 per element and another 4 figures for the skirmishers.

I decided I could produce the two armies from three boxes of plastic figures (total cost £15 to £20) as shown in the picture opposite, one of "Roman Infantry" (on the right), one of "Gaul Warriors" (on the left) and one of "Celtic Cavalry" (across the top). I ordered these online and a few days later they arrived through the post.

Historically the most famous of the battles between Romans and Germans was the disaster in the Teutoberger Wald when Varus was ambushed by the Germans and his three legions were destroyed. This is what happens when a Roman army is ambushed while marching in a column through thick forest. In other circumstances, they are much more equally matched and provide interesting confrontations.

Contents of three boxes of plastic figures

2.5 Preparing your Armies.

Having chosen and obtained your figures, the next step is to prepare and paint them. I prefer water-soluble paints, but others prefer enamels, such as those produced by Humbrol, or even oil paints. I have tried oil paints but find that they take too long to dry. If you do choose the Humbrol enamels or oil paints remember to buy some thinner as well so you can clean your brushes after each use. One advantage of water-based paints is that you can clean your brushes with water and do not need a special thinner.

A number of shops (such as W.H. Smiths or even some supermarkets in England) sell boxes with 12 to 18 tubes of paint and these usually provide a reasonable selection of colours. You should choose gouache or acrylic water-based paints because they are not transparent like the artists water colours and so you can overpaint one colour with another without the first colour showing through. My preference was for poster paints but Windsor and Newton have stopped producing them and the Reeves poster paints now have a limited selection of very bright garish colours. I have also found that the trial pots of emulsion paints can be mixed with the watercolours and I have been using the "terracotta" shade as a good flesh-coloured undercoat when diluted with a little water.

Other paints may be ordered online. Pelikan Plaka paints are still available and have a limited range of good colours for wargames figures. I have relied on their "Light Gold" and "Britannia Silver" for many years. Foundry Paint System has a very wide range of carefully designed colours. Other ranges are Coat d'armes paints (from Black Hat), Vallejo Colours, Army Painter, Miniature Paints (from Magnetic Displays), Citadel Paints (from Games Workshop) and Colour Party Paints who also supply "Basetex", a textured paint for covering the bases of your elements. These are all water-based paints designed for wargames. I cannot comment on them from my own experience because I am still using my large supply of poster paints.

Other places to buy paints of all types are the various craft shops and you will know better than I do what is available in your area. You will also need some fine brushes (both in size and quality) - again the art department of a High Street store is good for this. Choose brushes with a fine point and a variety of sizes - possibly number 2 and number 0 or 00 for the figures and a large, cheap one for varnishing and undercoating. (If you live in the U.S.A. you should go to your nearest Craft Store for all of the above.)

Opinions differ about undercoating. Some painters like a black undercoat and then use bright colours to pick out the details while others prefer a white undercoat. I have painted figures without any undercoat at all, but would not recommend this. One possibility is to use a white undercoat with enough Burnt Sienna (red-brown) paint mixed into it to produce a good flesh colour. Scantily-clad barbarians are quickly painted using a flesh-coloured undercoat. Rustoleum Plastic Primer Spray is recommended by some for use with plastic figures and this may be found at B & Q in England, Home Depot in USA and Bunnings in Australia. It is sold as an automotive product providing a white undercoat for plastic components.

Whatever your choice, you will need to prepare the figures and then attach them to temporary bases for painting. The figures are often slightly greasy when bought and so you will need to wash them thoroughly in the warm soapy water and it easier to do this while they are still attached to the sprue. I find one advantage of using water-based paints is that I can mix in a drop of washing-up liquid if I find the figure is still greasy and so the paint doesn't cover it.

Then you will need to cut the figures off the sprue using the modelling knife. Unless you are very much tidier than I am, you will need to protect the table on which you are working in some way - either a good thick wad of newspaper or plastic tray to work on. You will also need a small penknife or modelling knife and possibly a pair of clippers. If you are using water-based paints you will need a container for the water - I find a small jar used for fish paste or jam very good - small enough to be convenient and heavy enough that it is not easy to knock it over.

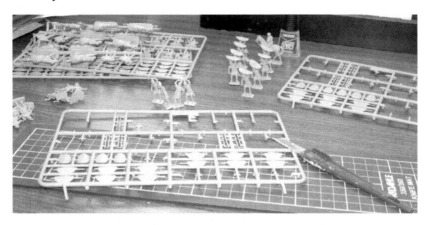

The picture shows the Roman army being cut from the sprue - note the Dahler Knife mat and the modelling knife in the foreground and the superglue in the back ground which has been used to attach the general to his horse and the shields to some of the troops. The mat protects the underlying table from damage when cutting the figures from the sprue and many model shops sell these along with other craft equipment.

You will need to use a suitable glue to attach the shields to the figures, some will need to have weapons attached and the cavalry will need to be attached to their horses. Then you will need to lay out all the figures and sort them out to decide which figures will belong to which element. Having made this decision, cut up your old cardboard box and attach the figures to the painting bases - one element per base with the figures well spread out to make them easy to paint.

For the "painting bases", I use an old cardboard box (such as the packet from a breakfast cereal) cut into strips and I attach all the figures for one element to one strip - either with "Blu-tak" or a small amount of PVA adhesive. The PVA adhesive may be used when one of the surfaces involved is a porous surface such as cardboard. If you need to stick metal to metal or plastic to plastic (for example attaching cavalry riders to their horses), then you will need a special purpose adhesive such as "Superglue". You will also need some sort of palette on which to mix your paints - for this I prefer china and use an old saucer or plate.

This picture shows the Roman army temporarily attached to its painting bases. The kit contained some beautifully modelled pila, but they were very flimsy and would not remain straight, so I decided to use pins instead. I took a pair of clippers and removed the head of the pin, then stuck it through the hole in the hand of the figure. It fitted loosely and would have fallen out, so I took the superglue and added a drop of glue to hold the pin to the figure's hand without (and this was the tricky part) getting ANY superglue on my own fingers. **This is very important**. Superglue sets quickly and joins any two surfaces, but is especially good at joining flesh to flesh.

While you are using Superglue, you need to have a Kleenex tissue handy and if you do get any on your fingers, you must **immediately** wipe them thoroughly with the tissue. This may result in fragments of paper tissue attached to your fingers, but that's better than having two fingers stuck together. If you let the glue dry fastening your fingers together, they will have to be sliced apart and that is a very delicate operation!

You will need to choose the most exuberant poses from the box of Celtic cavalry and paint each figure in different colours so that the element looks like wild irregular barbarians.

The bulk of the German army are the Warband - wildly individualistic and with as many different colours and poses as you can manage. With only three to a base, it is possible to arrange them in an irregular line on the base and make sure you don't have two figures in the same pose on the same base. This makes the army look very different from their opposing Roman army.

Finally the Psiloi are figures armed with javelins and placed two to a base. They differ from the Roman skirmishers in that they are not in uniform. These figures are prepared and attached to painting bases in the same way as the Roman army.

2.6 Painting the Armies.

Instructions for painting these figures can be found in *Armies and Enemies of Imperial Rome* by Phil Barker, which gives the full story for these and many other armies. Armies corresponding to small sections of this book have also been published by Osprey Books and if you use them, you will need to buy one book for each army you wish to use. The painting instructions here have been taken from Phil's book (with his permission).

Roman Legionaries of the late Republic.

"He wore a bronze helmet (Roman bronze was golden in colour like modern brass) and a long corselet of iron chain-mail. The horsehair crest in his helmet could have been natural black or dyed red, yellow or white. (I shall choose black for these troops because it gives a good contrast with the helmet colour.) His hair would also be black. His tunic would have been dyed red with madder (if you want to be extremely authentic, you can have each soldier with a slightly different shade of red because this fades with use or you can save time and paint them all the same scarlet). The centurion would have a different crest - in the colour of the unit (black in this case) and the standard-bearer would wear a bear-skin over his helmet."

"His long oval shield is dished and has a wooden centre spine on the outside which enlarges into a metal-covered boss protecting the central grip. It was made of plywood, covered and edged with thin leather and then painted with his unit's special pattern." (The plastic figures have an embossed pattern and for this unit, I chose to paint the shield black and then, after it had been varnished, I picked out the raised pattern in gold.)

"His main weapon was the pilum, a heavy throwing spear with a small head on a long iron rod which continued inside the wooden shaft to a considerable depth. It was thrown immediately before contact and had a good chance of penetrating the enemy's shield or armour and hanging there, hindering his movement if it failed to wound him. His other weapon was the gladius or sword, though they might also have had javelins to throw at a greater distance than the pilum."

Late Republican Cavalryman.

"He wears a mail corselet with wide shoulder straps and a bronze helmet with a yellow horse-hair crest. His tunic is either red like the infantry or possibly off-white with a coloured trim. His weapons are lance and javelins and he also has a long sword (called a spatha). His large round shield has a raised external rib like those of the infantry."

Horse Colours.

The most common colour for horses is known as "bay" (a brown horse with black trimmings - black mane, tail and lower legs). Also common is the "chestnut" - brown all over except for the "liver chestnut" which has pale mane and tail. The "dun" is a pale brownish-grey with black mane and tail and an "eel-stripe" of black along the spine. This was commoner in ancient times than it is today. Then there was the grey - dark grey when young (sometimes dappled) and fading as the animal ages until it becomes white.

Barbarian Symmachiarii.

"The mounted skirmishers are assumed to have been enlisted from other Gallic or German tribes and so they wear German costume but have Roman Shields."

Early German Infantry.

"The usual German garment was a cloak, which was sometimes their only garment apart from a loin cloth, although more often they wore close fitting trousers. Some wealthy men also had a tunic, but most of these would fight mounted. Hair styles varied, but most had blond or light brown hair. They had large shields in a variety of shapes, but most had a large boss which, like the Roman ones, could be used as an offensive weapon. Shields were brightly painted but clothing was dull - natural brown wool or dyed in dark greens, blues and browns. Swords were rare and highly prized - most Germans were armed with javelins or longer spears. The Warband and Psiloi would be dressed in the same way as each other, but the skirmishers would have javelins rather than longer spears. "

German cavalryman.

"These were usually members of the wealthiest class and would be dressed in tunic, trousers and cloak and would probably have a sword as well as the javelins and spears. They would have a brightly coloured round shield and might have a mail shirt and helmet." (The picture book "Asterix and the Goths" may also be used to give you ideas about painting these troops, both Roman and German.)"

The picture below shows the Roman Army painted and varnished and the German army partly painted. Once the paint is fully dry, I usually varnish the figures for added protection in use. The strongest varnish available is still the Humbrol gloss varnish, but I have found that clear nail varnish is almost as good and dries in seconds rather than hours. (If you intend to borrow this from female relatives, do ask their permission first.)

In the picture, you can also see the saucer used as a palette and the jar used for paint water as well as the two paint brushes, a fine one for painting the troops and an old thick one for varnishing.

2.7 Basing your Army.

Once the figures have been painted and varnished, it is time to mount them on their permanent bases. This is the point at which you need to decide on the scale to be used. In the next picture, the Roman army has been mounted on its permanent card bases while the German army is still on the temporary painting bases. In this example they are to be treated as 15mm figures, so all the bases are 40mm wide.

In the above example and using the standard smaller scale, the legionaries, mounted four to a base, are on bases 15mm in depth and are a very close fit. It is much easier if you choose figures in the same position so that they can fit closely together – in fact with this size of figures it is almost impossible to fit four figures into a base 40mm wide if they are not in the same position. The mounted troops are on bases 30mm in depth while the Psiloi have bases 20mm in depth. The extra figure to be placed in the camp (probably a wounded legionary in charge of the camp-followers) is also on a base 20mm in depth. Blank bases have been prepared for the German cavalry and camp-follower (30mm in depth for the cavalry and 20mm for the camp follower). All the rest of the German army, both psiloi and warband, are mounted on bases 20mm in depth.

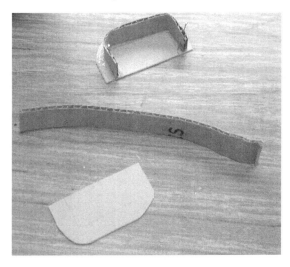

The last thing you need to prepare is the camp. There are many possible forms of camp, some of them real works of art. However the quickest and easiest is made with a piece of card for a base and a strip of corrugated card stuck to it.

The picture shows one of the camps with the corrugated card stuck to the base and a couple of pins holding it in position until the glue dries. The second one will be made in the same way.

Then it will need to be painted with a grey or pale brown undercoat and narrow random vertical stripes of various greys, browns and greens to give the impression of wooden posts – possibly some still with bark and leaves attached – and dark shadows between them.

The camp may be left empty, or be occupied by a camp-follower element or be occupied by one of the infantry elements of the army. An extra camp-follower element has been painted for each army and the Roman one is shown here.

Later all the bases, both of figures and of the camps, are smoothed over with filler (bought from a hardware store and intended for covering small cracks in the walls of a house before re-painting). This is applied with the modelling knife and the then finished with a paint brush dipped in water. Once this is dry, the bases are painted green to match the playing area.

The last two pictures show the two armies fully painted and ready for use. The Roman General is in the centre of his legions. The Roman light horse and cavalry have their shields painted to match the infantry.

A Roman DBA army

The German general appears on his white horse in the centre of the cavalry element. The nine elements of warband figures, three to a base, are in different exuberant poses while the psiloi and the camp are also present.

The complete German DBA army

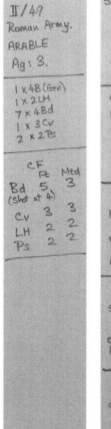

Finally I have made measuring sticks from strips of card.

On one side I have marked the BW measurements and also a reminder of which troops have which maximum move distance.

On the back I have copied information about the army including its terrain type and aggression, the exact army I have painted and a reminder of combat factors for use when they become engaged in mêlée.

Chapter Three: Making Your Terrain

Having produced your two armies, the next step is to produce the battlefield and its terrain. If you have chosen 15mm troops (as described in the previous chapter), you will need a playing area of approximately 600mm by 600mm (or 24 inches by 24 inches), while 25mm troops should have an area of 900mm by 900mm (or 36 inches by 36 inches).

3.1 Option One: Quick 'n' easy Terrain.

You will need to buy five green carpet tiles, a yard or metre of matt fawn braid and the same of shiny satin blue or green ribbon, both slightly less than 1 BW wide. The fawn braid may be used for roads and the blue ribbon for rivers. The battlefield and the road will be of long term use, but the others will need to be replaced later.

One easy method of making a battlefield is to use carpet tiles. In England (and the rest of Europe) carpet tiles are now decimal and so they are 500mm by 500mm. Previously, they were 12 inches by 12 inches and so four of them made an ideal *DBA* playing area for 15mm troops without any further work. In the new sizing, one carpet tile is too small for a playing area for 15mm while 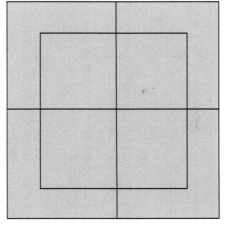 four carpet tiles are too large a playing area for 25mm troops. To obtain the correct size, you may either cut them down to size, which will leave pieces which can be used to make your hills or (as shown above) mark a playing area in the centre with a border round the edge to store casualties etc. This gives the basic playing area.

You will also need terrain features to place upon the battlefield. These come in two types – area terrain features and linear terrain features.

Area Terrain Features

These are things like hills and woods and so their size is defined by the smallest rectangle which may be drawn round the feature - as shown below. The length must be less than twice the width so very long thin features are not allowed.

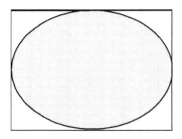

Also the maximum sum of length plus width allowed in the rules is 9 times the base width of the elements. So for 15mm troops, a large feature fits inside a rectangle of 200mm by 160mm (5 x 4 base widths). The smallest feature fits inside a square 40mm by 40mm.

Hills

You will need two types of hill – gentle hills and difficult hills. For this you should buy a fifth carpet tile and cut it into oval pieces of different sizes. Then a single extra piece of tile placed on the battlefield can represent a gentle hill while a heap of two or more pieces (in decreasing size) will give you a difficult hill.

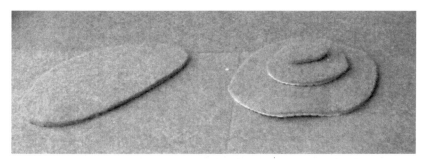

Woods & Rough Going

Turn over the piece of carpet tile prepared for the hill and the grey underside will do for the patch of rough going.

Since the ground inside a wood under the shade of the trees is often mainly bare earth, the same piece with a model tree placed upon it will represent a wood. Trees can be bought from model railway shops or downloaded from sites such a Junior General or Fiddlers Green.

Pendraken Games have a good supply of trees and so do Irregular Miniatures, though most of their terrain is at the smaller scales.

Linear terrain features.

The most usual examples of these are roads and rivers.

Roads run straight from one battle field edge to the opposite one and must be less than one base-width wide. The length of brown ribbon may be placed across the battlefield to represent this and will be good enough for long term use.

Rivers very seldom run in straight lines and so the blue or green ribbon will need to be replaced with something more realistic later on. Placing this blue ribbon along the edge of the battlefield can be used to indicate a waterway.

3.2 Option Two: Portable Terrain.

Many people make their battlefields on pieces of green cloth - either plain or decorated. A cloth battlefield may be crumpled up and used as padding when you pack your figures into a box to carry them around. The resulting creases will give the effect of natural features in the landscape whereas folding them tidily will give straight line folds which are most un-natural. If you paint the features on your battlefield, you cannot change it easily and so most players prefer to use a plain green cloth with models of the terrain features placed upon it.

I would love to be able to buy an air photo of an actual battlefield at the correct scale and printed on a suitable length of cloth. So far no-one has produced such an item, but I live in hope. In the meantime, it is possible to get a detailed map of a real battlefield and paint this on a piece of green or brown cloth if you want to reproduce an actual battle.

When I flew from England to New Zealand some years ago, I took a square of green cloth (shown here) on which I had painted the terrain features (giving a valid terrain for version 1.0 of *DBA* which was the version in use then). Roads and river are obvious and since I didn't expect to wash the cloth, I used poster paints for the roads, river and hills – I represented the hills by painting the area above each contour in a different shade – pale green, yellow ochre and finally a reddish-brown. When I reached New Zealand, I was accused of bringing a volcano about to erupt! This cloth is shown here with troops laid out on it.

If you have plenty of storage, you may wish to make a selection of permanent battlefields of plywood, polystyrene foam or other materials, painted in a variety of greens and browns to represent the countryside. Much of the scenery produced for model railways can also be used for battlefield terrain, in particular the coloured flock. It is possible to buy game mats for *DBA*, pre-cut to size and already flocked, so you don't need to make your own. If you visit local Home Improvement Stores, you may be able to buy off-cuts of carpet which may include suitable mottled green or brown designs.

3.3 Option Three: Realistic Terrain

Once you have got started on your wargaming, you will wish to produce more realistic terrain and this becomes more interesting to produce. Either a plain green or brown cloth or the four carpet tiles will make a good basis for the battlefield. This will represent the flat good going which covers most of the battlefield.

Gentle and Difficult Hills

One method uses a cardboard base, of the same card used for the figure bases- the gentle hill is cut to a curved shape within a rectangle of 4 x 3 base widths and the steep hill to one within a rectangle of 5 x 4 base widths. Then a polystyrene ceiling tile (available from DIY or Home Improvement Stores) is used for the main bulk of the hill. The ceiling tile is cut to the desired shape and then stuck to the card with PVA adhesive. One problem with these ceiling tiles is the large number of tiny spheres of polystyrene which are released when you cut the tile - they get everywhere and cannot be collected by a vacuum cleaner because they creep back out of the vacuum when it is switched off.

The best solution I have found (and it is not ideal) is to use a really sharp modelling knife or even a sharp pair of scissors to cut the ceiling tile (to minimise the number of spheres released) and then use a piece of parcel tape to collect them. They will stick to the tape and remain in place. This tape is then rolled up and thrown in the trash can.

The steep hill is prepared in the same way as the gentle one, but with several steps to make it higher. In this example, I have chosen to make one end of the hill very steep, with the steps close together, and the other end a much gentler gradient.

Once the slices of ceiling tile have been stuck to the card, they are covered with polyfiller to smooth out the steps and give the shape of a smooth hillside. At this point, some fine gravel is stuck into the steep hill to give the effect of rocky outcrops in the side of the hill. This is then left overnight to dry thoroughly. The filler will probably shrink slightly as it dries and so the steps will still be visible. A second coating will be needed to give a smooth surface to the hill.

Once the shape of the hill is correct, it will need to be painted in shades of greens and browns and possibly some flock added to give the effect of grass. You may also have wooded hills or rocky ones, other examples of "difficult hills".

Woods

The "wood" is another area terrain feature. This is often represented by a piece of brown card to indicate the area covered by the wood with two or three model trees standing upon it. A really tiny wood may only have room for one model tree, but most of them will need two or three. Many of the Early German armies have "Forest" as their home topography and so they will need several such woods. Woods count as "bad going" and Warband love fighting in bad going since this gives them an advantage against the Blades making up the legion.

The next picture shows a purpose-built wood for 15mm terrain. The top of the wood can be lifted up if you need to place troops under it.

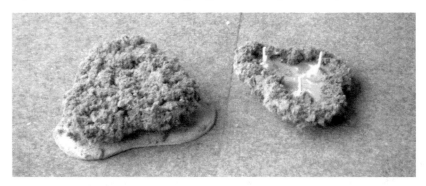

Since many woods have scrub round the edge, a base for the trees would be improved by a band of scrub around its edge. This is where the extra pieces of carpet tile which are no longer needed for hills can be re-used. Remove the carpet from the top and paint the surface in a green and brown patchwork. Then use some of the carpet stuck around the edge to produce this effect.

At one time, I attempted to produce some woods by dying some balls of cotton wool green and attaching them to a cardboard base. The result, seen on the front left of the picture overleaf, was not a success. However adding foliage (behind left) improved them greatly and with additional foliage round the edge (on the right) the end result was acceptable as a rather scrubby piece of woodland – with bushes rather than tall trees.

Rough Going

This is ground which is so difficult to get through that troops in such areas cannot remain in ordered ranks and so some troop types fight less well in these areas. Frequently this is an area of rocky ground and should be represented by a piece of cardboard or the base of a piece of carpet tile with some gravel stuck to it and painted accordingly.

The first picture shows two examples of rough. The one on the left uses the base of the carpet tile with a little of the carpet still stuck to it. The other one is intended for desert terrain and has gravel stuck to a card base and painted. The second picture shows more examples of rough, mostly with rocks and bushes and in one case with a large area of gorse or furze with its bright yellow flowers concealing the vicious thorns from the unwary.

Marsh

This is an area of wet land with deep enough pools to form a serious hazard to movement. Much of it will be bright emerald green, since many marsh plants are this colour and within it there will be deep pools (painted black with several coats of high gloss varnish to represent the water).

Marsh looks pretty, but can be dangerous. As a child, I lived on the North Yorkshire Moors (in England). This was during the Second World War and the British army used these moors for training. Near the village was a "bottomless bog" known and avoided by the locals. One of the tanks once drove into it and got stuck. They left it there overnight and came back in the morning with equipment to winch it out. However, during the night it had sunk slowly into the bog and it was never seen again. For all I know, it is still there.

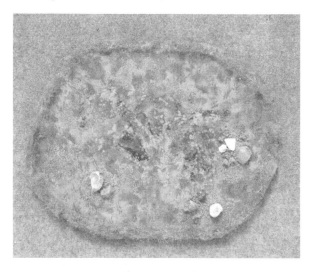

Roads

A road or track is an example of a "linear terrain feature" and must run from one battlefield edge to the one opposite. On the wargames table, roads run in a straight line from one side of the battlefield to the other and the "rolling English road" curving around the edge of hills, woods or ancient field boundaries is noticeably absent

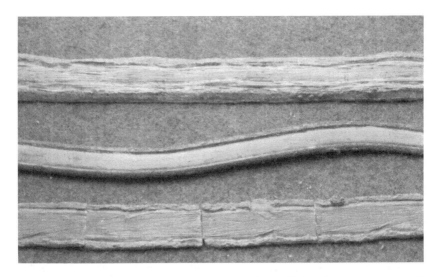

The road should be narrower than the width of an element and troops moving down the road should be placed so that they span it. Painting the edges green to match the carpet tiles will improve its appearance.

The examples in the photograph include some plastic models which will lie over hills and other terrain pieces as well as a single solid road and some road sections from Irregular Miniatures along the bottom. These do not curve over hills, but being in small sections, will follow the terrain to some extent.

Rivers and Waterways

The river Rhine is an example of a waterway – too big to be forded and with no bridges in the ancient period. The picture (taken on holiday in 1972) shows the Rhine below Drachenfels and here the water is brown with hints of blue. This means that the terrain needs to have the same colouring beneath something transparent such as a transparency intended for an overhead projector.

For a *DBA* battlefield alongside the river Rhine, the width of the waterway will not vary very much.

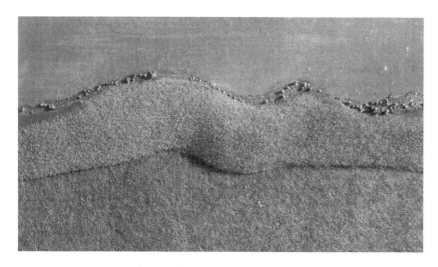

The maximum variation allowed in the rules is between 1 BW and 4 BW and less variation will probably look better. The waterway shown here has been painted on the underside of a transparency (so that the top is shiny) and had some translucent blue-green paint with a dark blue layer beneath it. It will take some experimentation to get a suitable effect.

Rivers and streams on the other hand do curve and this is usually reproduced on the wargames table. Consequently a length of blue ribbon is a poor representation of a river. You can prepare these in the same way as the waterway, but it's a lot of work and not really necessary when the sections sold by Irregular Miniatures give a good result and are much easier to produce.

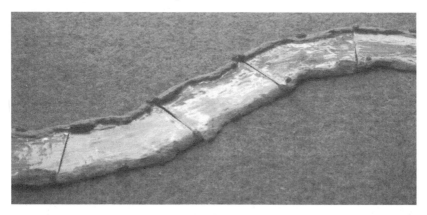

Dunes and Oases

Some armies may fight among sand dunes. Sand dunes form as heaps of sand in the distinctive crescent shape and you will need to build these upon a base of card. You could pile a heap of filler or modelling clay in top of this, but the resulting model will be very heavy. It is usually more convenient to use the same method for dunes as I have described for the hills.

You will need to buy some tiles and cut shapes to stick on the cardboard base and built up the rough shape of the dune. This will give a series of steps and you can then add the filler to smooth this over and fill in the steps, giving a smooth surface. Finally this can be painted to give a realistic colour. The result is shown on the front cover.

The oasis will be placed among the dunes. It consists of an oval piece of card with a small pool painted in the centre and a selection of bought palm trees clustered around it.

Built-Up Area (BUA)

There are four permitted types of BUA, namely City, Fort, Hamlet or Edifice. Each type has a slightly different effect under the rules and they are discussed here.

Type 1: A City.

Forget the urban sprawl of modern cities. Ancient cities were intended for defence and had strong walls surrounding them and often roads leading to them.

Some cities were too large to fit on the wargames table and so have to be modelled as a gateway and corner of the city walls placed on the edge of the table (assuming the rest of the city extends away off the table). A road will normally lead to the gateway.

Other cities may be placed on the battlefield and will therefore be limited to an area 4x5 BW like other area terrain features. (Two of the examples above are 3x3 BW and the smallest is 1x2BW. You don't get much of a city into this small size, but it is a valid piece of terrain.)

Ancient British armies may have their own hill-fort occupying the top of a steep hill – although they do not get extra tactical factors for the steep hill since this is included in the factor for the city. Many Spanish and Italian cities also occupy the tops of hills while others are placed in the bend of a river with extra strong walls covering the other sides. The picture shows a hill fort with a single entrance.

Top down view of a model of a British hill fort

Model of a Middle Eastern city with two gates

Other cities will have two or more city gates and in this case the rule allowing friendly elements to pass through them will apply. Both examples include a blank square in which an element intended as a garrison may be placed – the hill fort has a large enough space to include an element of slings or warband while the eastern city has enough room for an element of artillery should that be needed.

In each of these cases, I have used 6mm models to produce a city for use with 15mm troops. The picture below shows, on the right, four 15mm cataphracts as an element and on the left the much large number of 6mm troops to produce a similar element. The fact that the four 15mm figures or 3 rows of 6mm figures actually represent about 300 riders does not matter for the rules.

However, when you come to model a city, the fact that one model of a house represents 20 or 30 does look wrong. My first picture showed a single 15mm house inside a city wall, which is accurate for the scale, but I think the eastern city with its 6mm houses actually looks better on the battlefield. Admittedly the garrison of 15mm figures looks wrong in this scale of city and you might want to have alternative models of 6mm figures for your garrisons.

Irregular Miniatures offer a wide range of terrain pieces in 6mm scale and also in the even smaller 2mm scale. The picture on the next page shows some of their woods and a pond as well as a 2mm Ancient British camp. I have occasionally used this 2mm camp as an isolated farmstead forming a hamlet.

Type 2: A Fort.

The model shown here could be either a city or a castle. The bailey would have been occupied by many temporary structures such as market stalls or enclosures for cattle or horses.

Type 3: The hamlet

Farms and fields may be added to the scenery, but will have no effect on the combat. We have several pieces of cloth printed with a pattern of cultivated fields and these may be placed on the battlefield to make it look more realistic. They may even be accompanied by farm cottages of the correct period, forming a hamlet.

Type 4: Edifice.

This type was added after observing some players had beautiful models of pyramids, temples, the Ark of the Covenant etc. which add to the appearance of the battlefield but did not previously appear in the rules. These now appear under the title "edifice" and count in the battle as "rough going" or may be included in the camp if the player so wishes.

Camps

If you have not chosen have a BUA, then your army must have a camp. This is a temporary fortification placed on your base line at the start of the game. It must have an area large enough to contain one element of infantry within a wall or an earthen bank. You may choose to garrison it with one of your twelve elements or you may paint a "camp-follower" element to leave in your camp. The pictures show a number of examples of camps for *DBA* armies.

The first picture shows a selection of 15mm camps painted and ready for use. The next has three 15mm scale camps and one 25mm camp. Three of these are made from sections of wall stuck to a cardboard base and then painted. The fourth, intended for a Mongol army, has tents and horses stuck to a suitable base.

Finally here is the Roman camp described in chapter two with its "camp follower" element (a Roman soldier recovering from his wounds who has been left behind in the camp). The German camp was made in a similar way.

If you continue to play wargames, you will probably wish to produce more and more different types of terrain for the various armies you produce. There are a number of sources selling cardboard buildings which are light to carry around from place to place.

One of these is "Fiddlers' Green" (found online at *www.fiddlersgreen.net*) which are cheap and cheerful and have a very wide range of models. Some of the colours may be a bit garish, but as you download and print them, you should be able to tone down the colours before printing if this is your preference. Since you print them out, you can choose which scale you want.

Another is "Paper Terrain" (shown here), a much more upmarket product, but with few ancient buildings. Details may be found at *www.paperterrain.com* and the range of models is increasing all the time. The buildings are sold in groups and some can be a bit fiddly to complete, but the end result is well worth the trouble. The picture shows some of the buildings from their modern Arab village with each house and out-buildings mounted on a separate base with walls to enclose a compound as will be found in some villages in Afghanistan. Paper terrain actually include two copies of each building - the one as you see it and underneath it a ruined version in case it is destroyed in the wargame (not applicable to an ancient game).

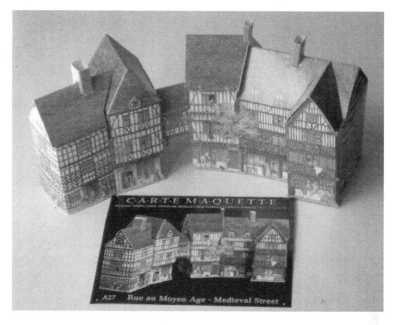

"Carte Maquette" by Editions Mirontaine is another source of cardboard models. Information may be found on their website *www.mirontaine.com* and they appear to be based in Bordeaux, France. I cannot remember where I found this example of a Medieval Street.

Another source, not intended for wargames terrain but still useful, is the Usborne books of cut-out models. These may be found at *www.usborne.com* and then look for "cut-out models". There are a wide range of models, many of them useful for *DBA*. The range includes Roman fort, Roman villa, Viking village, medieval village, medieval town, castle and cathedral. Other books in the series are less suitable for *DBA* such as the wizard's castle, dinosaurs, Egyptian mummy, Trojan Horse and wild-west fort. Others may be added from time to time.

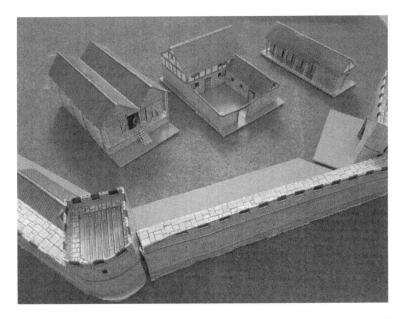

Each book contains a complete item such as a Roman Marching Camp (seen here) and if you make it up stuck to the single painted base as they intend, it is too restricted to be of very much use for wargames terrain. However, if you mount each building (or section of wall) on a separate base, you will have some very useful buildings.

Then there are many solid models which only need to be painted. One example is shown here. Some of them are excellent in both scale and detail. I particularly like "Hovels", who have a catalogue with a large collection of buildings in a variety of periods and scale, all advertised on their website _www.hovelsltd.co.uk_ . You can also buy battlefields, hills, rivers, sand dunes etc.

Some are found in craft or model shops intended for model railways, others are meant for fantasy wargaming. And of course, the dealers' room at a show like *Historicon* will provide endless temptation.

Finally this example, from the Shrewsbury Wargames Society, shows a painted background behind a pair of terrain boards.

Chapter Four: Playing a Game.

The earlier chapters have discussed making the army and the terrain. Now the time has come to play a game, using the two armies described earlier. The Roman player will be called "*Marcus*" and his German opponent will be called "*Hermann*". Don't expect good tactics in this game because they are newcomers to DBA and are finding out how to play the game by referring back to the rules at frequent intervals.

Creating the Battlefield

First the players must decide who is the invader and who is the defender. For this, they will need to use their dice. Marcus proudly produced his "Roman dice" with Roman numerals on each face.

"That's not a PIP dice." objected Hermann "It doesn't have any pips."

"That doesn't matter." replied Marcus "It's a Roman dice and I'm a Roman."

After some discussion, Hermann agreed reluctantly, but still considered that the German dice, with a different pattern of pips on each face, was the only proper PIP dice (as recommended in the rules).

Marcus then threw his dice and scored a II (2). Adding this score to the aggression of 3 for the Roman army gave him a total of 5.

Hermann also scored 2 on the dice, but the German aggression was only 2, giving a total of 4.

Since the Roman army had the higher total, Marcus was the invader.

"Since I'm the defender, I get to choose the terrain" said Hermann.

"That's right" replied Marcus "You can have one or two compulsory features and two or three optional ones".

They laid out four carpet tiles to form the battlefield, one tile for each quarter. The numbers one to four shown in the picture on the next page are used to explain how the battlefield was produced.

"I'm a German and so my terrain type is Littoral", said Hermann. "I thought Germans always lived in the forest" objected Marcus. "I'm one of the Cherusci" replied Herman, "That means I always fight you on the banks of the mighty river Rhine, which counts as a waterway. My compulsory terrain feature is a waterway and I'm only allowed the one. I have to place it along one edge and I shall need to dice and see which one".

The dice throw was a 1 and so the waterway was placed along the edge joining quarters one and two. This was Hermann's choice – he could equally well have placed it along the edge joining quarters one and four.

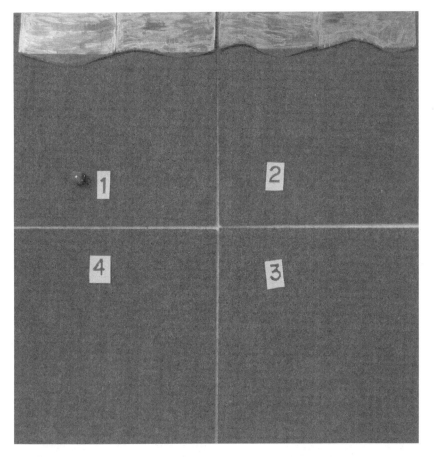

Initial view showing waterway and playing area divided into 4.

"Your optional features are marsh or difficult hills, woods or dunes, BUA, river or road" said Marcus.

"I know" said Hermann "and I choose three woods, two large and one slightly smaller."

For the first wood, a large one, the dice throw was a 3 and Hermann placed the wood in the third quarter near the centre of the battlefield. For the next wood, the smaller one, the dice throw was a 6.

"Oh good" said Marcus, "that means I can choose the quarter. I choose number two. It's a close fit and if there isn't enough room to place it you'll have to discard it".

Hermann laid the wood down in the corner of the square furthest from both the waterway and the large wood and measured carefully.

"Look" he said "luckily it was the small wood and there is **just** one BW between the waterway on one side and the large hill on the other. So I can place it in this position". Marcus checked the measurements and agreed it was correct.

The dice for the final wood was a 5 allowing Hermann to decide where to place it and he duly placed in the fourth quarter.

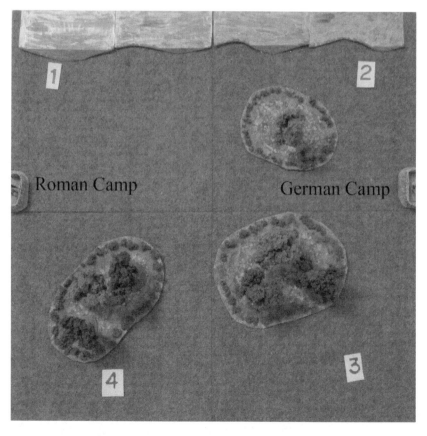

Complete battlefield with terrain and camps.

Deployment

"Now" said Marcus "I choose my base edge. I think I like that one." He pointed at the edge joining sides 3 and 4.

"You can't have it" replied Hermann "There's no road and so you are not allowed to choose the edge opposite a waterway. You cannot force me to set up in the middle of the waterway and drown my army before it gets a chance to fight. You can choose the waterway as your base edge if you like but you cannot force me to use it."

"In that case" said Marcus, indicating the edge joining 1 and 4, "I might as well choose this one" and he placed his camp in the centre of the edge.

"That's fine" said Hermann and placed his camp in the centre of the opposite edge. Both camps were occupied by camp followers keeping all twelve elements of both armies on the battlefield. The result is shown on the previous page.

Since there was no city or fort on the battlefield, most of the troops had to be placed within a rectangle 3BW from the centre line and 4BW from the sides, which is indicated by the white lines on the next picture. The Light Horse, Cavalry and Psiloi could be within a larger rectangle only 2BW from the sides of the battlefield, i.e. they could extend into strips on either side of the marked rectangle.

As the defender, Hermann had to place his army first and he placed seven Warband elements in the large wood, two in the small one and his General in between the woods

"You've missed two" said Marcus helpfully.

"No I haven't" said Hermann mysteriously "I've got plans for them. You'll find out in due course".

Marcus was puzzled since DBA doesn't allow for ambushes or flank marches, but decided not to bother about it. He then deployed his army with the eight legionary elements of Blades in a block alongside the wood and as far forward as possible. His General was in the back rank of the legion. The two Psiloi elements were in the wood. The Cavalry and the Light Horse, who could be within 2BW of the edge were in a column on the extreme right and as far forward as possible without entering the wood. Marcus intended to send the Cavalry and Light Horse round the flank and behind the woods to attack the German General in the rear.

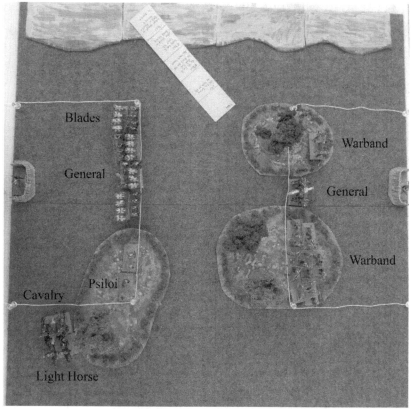

The battlefield with the two deployment areas marked out and the troops in position.

German First Bound

As defender, Hermann had the first bound. Before he threw his PIP dice, Hermann placed his two elements of Psiloi in a group touching the bank of the river Rhine.

"What are you doing?" asked Marcus.

"My home terrain type is Littoral" replied Hermann "so I can reserve two or three elements for a river landing to be deployed in my first move anywhere along the waterway. I choose to deploy my two Psiloi elements. I can place them anywhere along the river but I choose to place them close to your baseline."

Marcus was alarmed that he had failed to allow for this, but comforted himself that they were only Psiloi who couldn't do much damage.

Hermann threw his PIP dice and scored a 3. He used all his PIPs to move the Psiloi. Since they were beyond command distance from his General, he would normally need two PIPs per move but not in his first bound. Since they were Psiloi, he could move them twice in the first bound.

First he moved the entire group 3BW towards the Roman camp using his first PIP. Then he moved one element of Psiloi into position attacking the camp from the front. Finally he moved the second element of Psiloi into position attacking the side of the camp.

"You can't do that" said Marcus.

"Why not? " asked Hermann.

"A second tactical move must not go within 1 BW of the enemy" explained Marcus.

Hermann checked in his set of rules and then moved the Psiloi back and placed them side by side as a group just 1 BW from the side of the camp. Since the Psiloi were now still in the group in which they started the move, this only required 2 PIPs. Hermann did not use the third PIP.

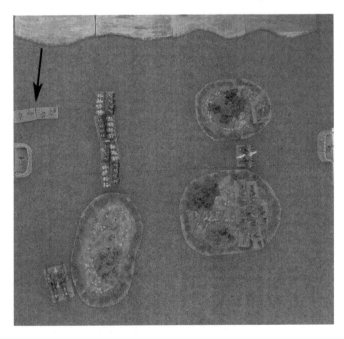

End of German First Bound.

The change was permissible since it was replacing an illegal move with a legal one. As with chess, once a legal move has been made and the element placed, the player is committed to that move. A legal tactical move can only be changed if the initial position was marked and the opponent consents.

Roman First Bound

Marcus threw his PIP dice and scored a V (5).

Since he wished to move the whole group of blades closer to the waterway, he used one PIP to rotate the whole group. The front left-hand corner of the group was the pivot and the front right-hand corner moved forward 2BW.

He used one PIP to move the group of the Light Horse and Cavalry 4BW along the outside of the wood and then a second PIP to move the Light Horse an extra 4BW.

He used his remaining two PIPs to move one element of Psiloi two moves back to face the German Psiloi threatening the camp.

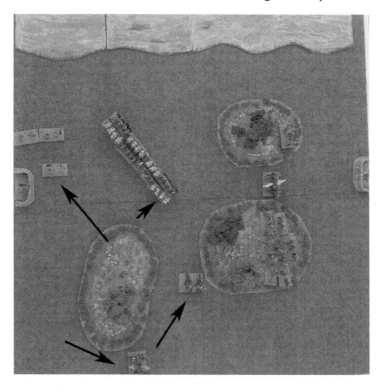

End of Roman First Bound

German Second Bound

Hermann's PIP dice was only a 2 which limited his options. He chose to move the group of Psiloi, which were more than the command distance of 8BW from his general and so required an extra PIP to move them, into contact with the Roman Psiloi.

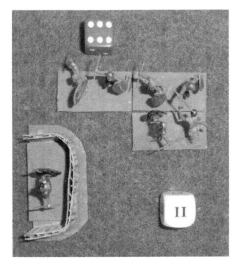

Having moved the group straight forward until their front edges touched the front edge of the Roman element, he then slid the group sideways to conform with the enemy and ended with one element lined up with the Roman and the other as an overlap.

For any combat, the elements involved have be in front-edge to front-edge contact and also have their front corners in contact. However psiloi, unlike other types of troops, are not allowed to claim the second element as an overlap.

This resulted in the first combat of the game. Hermann threw a 6 for his combat dice but Marcus could only throw a II (2).

German Psiloi had a basic 2 plus 6 for the dice.

Germans: 2 + 6 = 8

The Roman psiloi had a basic 2 plus 2 for the dice.

Romans 2 + 2 = 4

The Roman Psiloi had scored half the German total and so they were destroyed. Marcus was appalled.

Roman Second Bound

Marcus was even more appalled when he threw his movement dice and only scored 1. Since he could not intervene to assist the camp, he decided to move the group of Blades forward another 2BW towards the Germans.

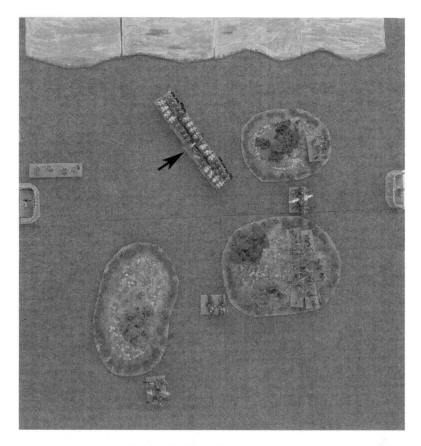

End of Roman Second Bound

German Third Bound

Hermann now threw his movement dice and scored 4. He used them to attack the Roman camp with his two Psiloi elements. One element was moved into contact with the side of the camp (using 2 PIPs). The other was moved in to contact with the front of the camp (using the other 2 PIPs).

First both sides threw their combat dice, for the combat between the first element of Psiloi attacking the side of the camp and the camp follower defending the camp.

The Roman had a basic factor of 2 plus an extra 2 for defending the camp. He was minus 1 for the second Psiloi element also attacking the camp. His dice throw was III (3) and so his total was

$2 + 2 - 1 + 3 = 6$

The German had a basic factor of 2 and his dice was 4 giving

$2 + 4 = 6$

The scores were equal and so this combat continued.

Next they evaluated the combat with the second Psiloi element attacking the front of the camp. This time the Roman's dice was again a 3 but the German scored a 5 (as shown in the next picture).

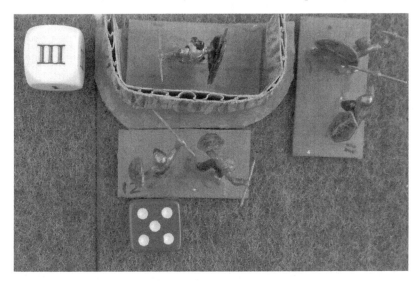

German Bound 2 combat 2

Once again the Roman had a basic factor of 2 plus an extra 2 for defending the camp. He was minus 1 for the second Psiloi element still attacking the side of camp. His dice throw was III (3) and so his total was

$2 + 2 - 1 + 3 = 6$

This time the German had a basic factor of 2 plus 5 for the dice

$$2 + 5 = 7$$

End of German Bound 2

This meant that the Roman total was less and so the camp follower was destroyed and the winning German Psiloi entered the camp and sacked it.

Roman Third Bound

Marcus was dismayed to lose his camp, but a score of V (5) on his PIP dice was a little comfort.

He used 1 PIP to rotate the Blades forward again. this time using the front right-hand corner as a pivot and moving the front left-hand corner 2 BW forward.

He used another PIP to move his remaining Psiloi out of the wood towards the camp.

"I'll use my remaining 3 PIPs to move the Light Horse three moves back to support the Psiloi" said Marcus "I know command distance is only 4BW for the Cavalry hidden behind the wood, but these are Light Horse and so their command distance is 20BW. They are well within that".

Hermann agreed and so Marcus used the remaining 3 PIPs to move the Light Horse 3 times. The situation is shown in the picture on the next page.

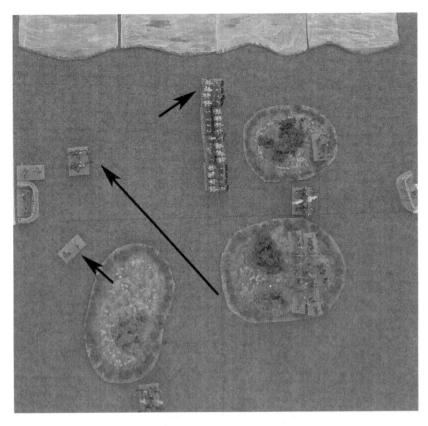

End of Roman Third Bound

German Fourth Bound

Now it was Hermann's turn to have bad luck and throw a 1 for his movement dice. Since the Psiloi were still more than 8BW from his General, he would have needed 2 PIPs to move each of them.

Instead he moved one of the Warband from the large wood towards the small one to join their friends in case the Romans entered the wood to attack them.

Roman Fourth Bound

Marcus threw II for his PIP dice, but this was enough to attack the Psiloi and revenge the camp.

For 1 PIP he moved the Light Horse to attack the second element of Psiloi in the flank. They could do this because they were

beyond an imaginary line drawn along the side edge of the element to be attacked. The Light Horse had to line up with the front edge of the Light Horse in contact with the side edge of the Psiloi and with the two front corners in contact.

The other PIP was used to attack the Psiloi who had been sacking the camp. Since the sacked camp gave no tactical advantage to troops occupying it, it was removed from the battlefield at this point and put with the other casualties. The German Psiloi remained in the same position facing the edge of the battlefield until they were contacted in the rear by the Roman Psiloi.

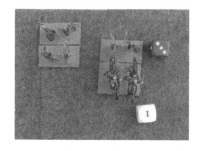

Both German elements then had to turn and face their attackers for the two combats.

Since it was Marcus' bound, he could choose the order in which the combats were fought. He chose to fight the Light Horse first.

He was unlucky in this combat, the Romans threw I and the Germans 3.

The Light Horse had a basic factor of 2, plus 1 for the dice.

$2 + 1 = 3$

German Psiloi had a basic factor of 2 plus 3 for the dice.

$2 + 3 = 5$

The Light Horse had scored less than their opponents and had to recoil, moving back their base depth.

The next combat reversed the outcome; Marcus threw VI and Hermann 1.

The Roman Psiloi had a basic factor of 2 plus 6 for the dice

$2 + 6 = 8$

The German Psiloi had a basic factor of 2 plus 1 for the dice.

$2 + 1 = 3$

The German score was less than half that of the Romans and so the Germans were destroyed.

German Fifth Bound

Hermann threw 4 on his dice. He could do nothing to help the surviving Psiloi. Although the Psiloi were not currently in contact with the Light Horse, they were inside their Threat Zone and so could only move directly away from them or forward into contact. If they moved away, they would leave the battlefield and count as lost.

Therefore he used these PIPs to tidy up the position in the wood in preparation for the Roman attack. He decided to line up where the two woods were only one BW apart. He moved all four elements small distances and finished up with the General next to the large wood and the three Warband elements in line with him inside the small wood. This is shown in the next picture.

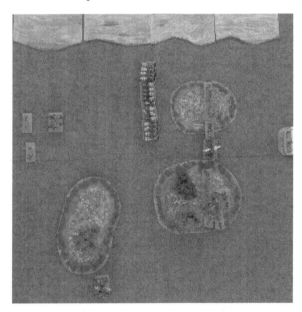

End of German Fifth Bound

Roman Fifth Bound

Marcus threw a VI on his PIP dice. He split the large group into two, using one PIP to move the group of six elements of Blades forward until it touched the edge of the wood. He used another PIP to move the column of two Blades forward the full 2 BW.

He used two of these PIPs to attack the German Psiloi, moving the Light Horse back into contact and the Roman Psiloi into the overlap position.

He used the final 2 PIPs to move the Cavalry one move, bring them back into the command distance. While they had been hidden behind the wood, command distance had been reduced to 4BW.

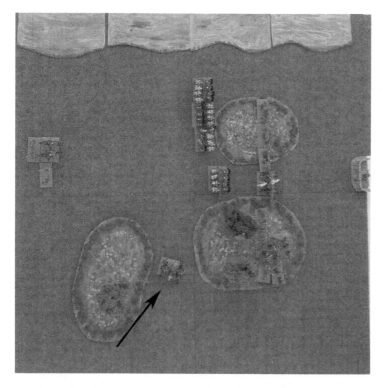

End of Roman Fifth Bound.

The German Psiloi combat dice was a 3 giving a basic combat factor of 2 minus 1 for the overlap and plus 3 for the dice, a total of 4.

The Roman combat dice was a VI, so the Light Horse had a basic combat factor of 2 plus 6 for the dice giving a total of 8.

$$6 + 2 = 8$$

The German Psiloi's total was half that of its opponent so they were destroyed.

German Sixth Bound

Now Hermann again threw 1 on his PIP dice. He could have moved his General back out of danger and then replaced him with a warband element in the next bound, but he thought the General should fight in the front rank. Normally this would be correct.

He could have moved a warband element to line up with the General and provide an overlap when the General was in combat. This would have been a very good idea.

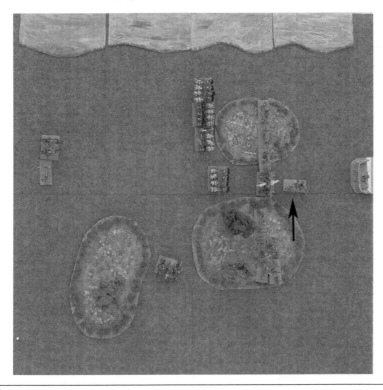

Instead he decided to try and move one warband unit along the behind the line and into position on the far flank, to prevent the Romans having an overlap. So he used his single PIP to move another Warband out of the large wood towards the small one.

Roman Sixth Bound

Marcus rolled V for his PIP dice and used 4 PIPs to move four elements of Blades into the wood. This is where Marcus made his big mistake. He knew that the Blades had a tactical factor of 5 against the Warband's factor of 3 and thought this gave him enough of an advantage to deal with the two Warband elements in the wood, even though they couldn't claim rear support in the wood. He knew they couldn't move as a group, so that he had to use all his 4 PIPs to move the 4 single elements into the wood. He forgot that woods are bad going which imposes an extra tactical factor of -2 on solid foot such as Blades.

Then he used his last PIP to move an element of Blades from the second rank forward towards the German General.

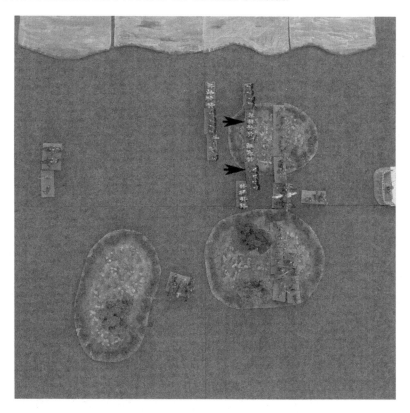

German Seventh Bound

Hermann threw yet another 1 and moved the Warband into the small wood behind his front line.

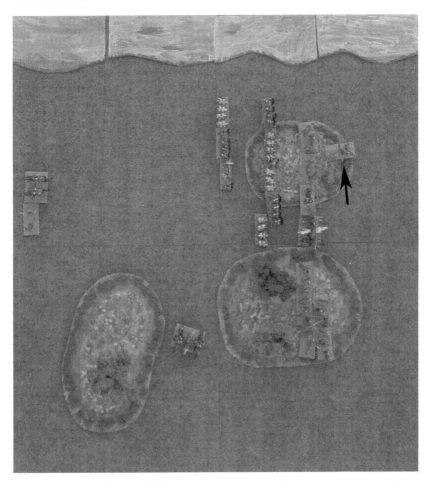

Roman Seventh Bound

Once again the Romans threw V for their movement dice. Marcus moved five single elements of Blades forward to contact the Germans.

This resulted in four combats.

Since it was the Roman bound, Marcus could choose in which order the combats were fought and he chose to fight the one on his left (at the top of the picture) first.

Combat dice were thrown. The Romans scored 1 and the Germans 4.

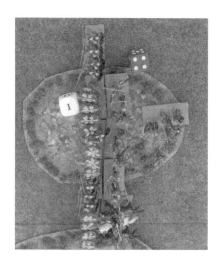

The Roman Blades had a basic factor of 5 against foot, they were -2 because they were fighting in bad going and had 1 on the dice.

Roman total was 5 -2 +1 = 4

The German Warband had a basic factor of 3 against foot, were minus 1 because they were overlapped by the second element of Romans and had 4 on the dice.

German total was 3 -1 + 4 = 6

The Romans had scored less and were fighting Warband, so they were destroyed. The Warband they had been fighting had to pursue by moving half a BW straight ahead, as shown below.

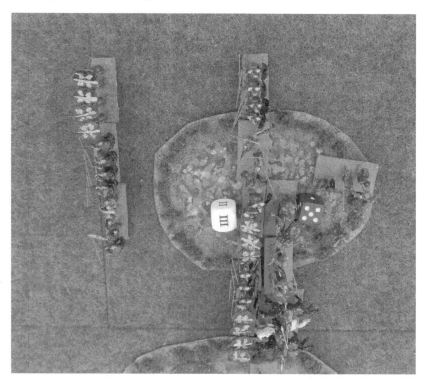

Second Combat

Then they fought the second combat. Again Marcus could choose and might have been wiser to choose the third from the top, but he decided to move in sequence from left to right. This time, the Romans threw III (3) and the Germans 5.

The Roman Blades were again a basic factor of 5 and a tactical factor of -2 since they were in bad going and another minus 1 for the overlapping Warband (side edge in contact with side edge also counts as an overlap) so:

Roman total was $5 - 2 - 1 + 3 = 5$

The German Warband was again a basic factor of 3 and had 5 on the dice.

German total was $3 + 5 = 8$

The Romans had scored less and were destroyed and again the Warband had to pursue.

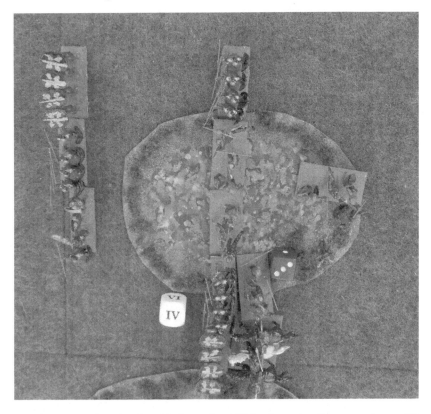

Then they fought the third combat. This time the Romans threw IV and the Germans threw 3 on their combat dice.

The Romans scored 5 -2 -1 + 4 = 6

The Germans scored 3 + 3 = 6

"A tie" said Hermann "that means we carry on".

"No" replied Marcus "the Blades are Solid foot and the warband are Fast foot. This means that the warband have to recoil one base depth and the Blades follow up for half a base width, ending in contact again. This means that this combat will continue into the next Bound."

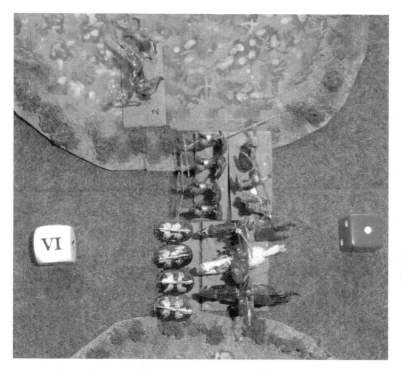

Finally came the combat involving the German General, the fatal one for Hermann as it turned out. The Romans threw VI and the Germans 1. Such dice score combinations are very rare and usually fatal. This time was no exception.

The Roman Blades had a basic score of 3 against mounted troops plus 6 on the dice.

Roman 3 + 6 = 9

The German General, being Cavalry, had a basic score of 3 plus 1 for the General minus 1 for the overlap and plus 1 for the dice.

German $3 + 1 - 1 + 1 = 4$

The German General had scored less than half his opponent's score and so he was destroyed. Hermann was dismayed and Marcus jubilant.

In fact, if Hermann had moved a warband into position alongside the General, the Roman score would have been only one less due to the overlap and it would not have changed the result. The dice had favoured the Romans throughout this game.

At the end of this bound, The Romans had lost their camp (counts as 1 element destroyed) an element of Psiloi and 2 elements of Blades – a total of 4

The Germans had lost their General (counts as 2 elements destroyed) and 2 elements of Psiloi – also a total of 4.

Since neither side had lost more, the battle continued. The next losses would determine the outcome.

German Eighth Bound

The German PIP dice was a 3. Since the General had been lost, Hermann needed an extra PIP for each tactical move – this meant he could move one single element and the third PIP could not be used.

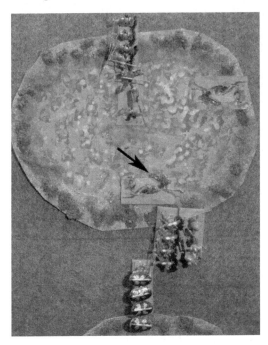

He decided to attack the Roman still in combat with the Warband in the flank by moving the nearest Warband in a single element move.

He rotated it through 90 degrees and then moved to contact the side edge of the Roman with his front edge and moved along so that the two front corners were in contact.

Since the movement of the Warband was not hindered by being in the wood, he had the full 3BW move and was able to do this.

Had the Roman wished to make a similar attack, the movement of the Blades would have been limited to 1BW inside the wood and would have needed two moves to complete this manoeuvre.

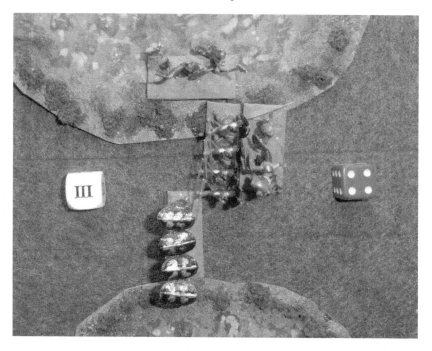

They threw the dice for this combat, the vital result which would decide the game. The Roman score was III and the German was 4.

The Roman had a basic factor of 5, less 2 for the wood, less another one for the Warband overlapping on the flank and plus 3 for the dice.

Roman $5 - 2 - 1 + 3 = 5$

The German had a basic factor of 3 plus 4 for the dice.

German $3 + 4 = 7$

So the German score was higher and the Roman was destroyed.

This meant that at the end of this bound:-

The Romans had lost their camp (counts as 1 element destroyed), an element of Psiloi and 3 elements of Blades – a total of 5.

The Germans had lost their General (counts as 2 elements destroyed) and 2 elements of Psiloi – a total of 4.

So the German General had achieved a posthumous victory!

As Is the custom in DBA play, they finished by shaking hands.

Later they played another game in which each avoided the mistakes of this game – but made new and more interesting ones.

Chapter Five: De Bellis Antiquitatis Rules version 3.0

5.1 Introduction

NOTE: The *DBA* rules have been developed by my husband Phil Barker and myself and are included here with his permission.

DBA is an ancient and medieval period wargame played on a small board, using a minimal number of model figures and the simplest set of rules that can produce a historically and visually realistic and exciting game.

Its genesis was an experimental set for battles between Romans and Celts demonstrated by Phil at the 1988 Society of Ancients conference. This led to a more general two-page rule set called *De Bellis Societatis Antiquorum* used for a knock-out competition to be played in the small gaps between events at the 1989 conference. In 1990, a commercial version *De Bellis Antiquitatis 1.0* was produced which extended the combat system, added a few extra troop types, and included fuller explanation of procedures and philosophy than had been possible in two pages and incorporated set-up information and army lists for more than 300 ancient and medieval armies. This was developed further and replaced by later versions. A selection of these early versions may be purchased from John Curry as part of *The History of Wargaming Project*, under the title *DBA 2.2*.

The order of the sections in these rules is that in which they are used. It starts with definitions, then army preparation, then terrain preparation, then the actual battle rules in the order in which they are usually needed.

Our original intent was to provide the simplest possible set of wargames rules that retain the feel and generalship requirements of ancient or medieval battle. The rule mechanisms started from the assumptions that the results of command decisions could be shown rather than the minutia of how orders were communicated and interpreted, that the proportions of different troops fielded were decided by availability within their culture and not cost-effectiveness against the current opponent, that differences between troops of the same class and era were relatively unimportant, and that most shooting regardless of theoretical weapon range was at very short distances. The resulting system is more subtle than may be immediately apparent, and is the fruit of much detailed development.

The general idea is that a wargame should look like and provide the tension of a real battle, that players should have only the information and command capabilities that a real general would have, that simplicity is a virtue, and that players should win by realistic tactics, not by bureaucratic manipulation of army composition or inherently slow analysis of the rules. The objective is the mind of your opponent and speed helps apply pressure.

The best way to learn to play is from a kindly experienced opponent. The example game in chapter four gives a bound-by-bound account of a battle and is another good way to learn how *DBA* works. Failing these, put two simple armies down and play both sides until you are familiar with the concepts

A game usually lasts less than an hour, so that a six-round convention competition can be completed in one day and still leave plenty of time for visiting the trade stands. Since most battles end in outright victory, the organiser's work is minimised.

DBA version 3.0 is the result of a thorough revision process by a large panel that included *DBA* competition organisers and umpires on three continents and has been available for open testing on line. Some changes are only to improve clarity. Others eliminate geometrical ploys beloved of some gamesmen that have no historical basis. In particular, troops that would contact or shoot at each other in real life must now also do so in the game. Yet other changes improve historical balance by giving troops of the same type slightly different capability when they are depicted differing by basing or bow type.

Wargame rules often favour methodical safety-first generals, while in real war commanders with flair often out-perform them. A new method of measuring distances helps to simulate this by encouraging the use of a reserve to exploit opportunities more easily and making it harder to hide vulnerable troops out of reach at the rear.

The period covered has been extended up to 1520 to take in the early part of the Great Italian Wars and the Ottoman-Mamluk wars. The fully revised army lists include extra description to inspire beginners. Few lists necessitate changes to an existing army, but many have additional options that add to the richness of the game.

5.2 Design Philosophy

The *DBA* command system appears arbitrary, but gives results very similar to those of more elaborate systems using written orders, transmission by messenger or signal and testing of interpretation on receipt. It also substitutes for the testing of troops' reaction to events and effectively simulates loss of cohesion in battle.

Wargamers pay more attention to weaponry than did real commanders. Surviving ancient manuals lump all foot skirmishers as psiloi whether armed with javelins, sling or bow, defining them by function rather than armament. We have applied the same principle throughout with no apparent loss of overall realism. Morale and training distinctions have also been discarded as linked with function. Thus, most knights are rash, all warbands are fierce but brittle, and all skirmishers are timid.

Phil Barker playing DBA at Historicon.

Similarly, a real general did not know a unit's losses until next day, if then. However, he would be able to see if a body was advancing cheering, standing its ground, edging back looking over its shoulders or had broken in rout. We provide players with that information and that only. Victory as well as realism under these rules is most likely to be achieved by thinking of elements as bodies of real troops rather than playing pieces, and using them historically.

5.3 Playing Equipment & Representational Scales.

Choice of Figure and Model Scale.

These rules can be used with any scale of figure or model, but two scales are usual. The larger uses a base width (BW) of 60mm with nominally 25mm (actually 20-28mm) figures. The smaller uses a 40mm base width with nominally 15mm (actually 10-20mm) figures. 15mm has been the most usual scale since it combined cheapness with convenience. The larger scale offers easier visibility for spectators and opportunity for more detailed painting and is gaining in popularity with the availability of cheaper plastic figures. Greater numbers of 6mm or 2mm figures can be substituted for either scale.

Playing Area.

The standard playing area, "the battlefield", is square; with sides 600mm/24" to 800mm/32" for the smaller scale and 900mm/36" to 1,200mm/48"square for the larger scale. Be warned that areas larger than the minimum are unnecessary and may encourage overly defensive play or result in longer or even unfinished games. It is usually assembled from separate terrain features placed on a flat base, but a single integral terrain block or grouped quarter-size blocks, may be provided instead by competition organisers; if so, they must avoid making the terrain too symmetrical or uniform.

Army Size and Troop Representation.

An army consists of 12 elements as specified in their army list, one of which includes its only general. Others can sometimes be replaced by elements of another army listed as allied. The army must also have either a camp or a city and can have both. These can be occupied by 1 of the 12 elements of its own army list, or by camp followers or city denizens additional to the 12

An element consists of a thin rectangular base of card or similar material, to which is fixed figures (or the equivalent 6mm or 2mm blocks) typically representing 6 to 10 ranks of close-formed foot, 4 or 5 ranks of most mounted troops or of skirmishers, or a single rank of elephants, scythed chariots, artillery or wagons. It nearly always has the same size and number of figures as corresponding DBMM elements, but represents more men.

The number of men represented by a single element varies according to the size of army simulated, but is always at least twice that in DBMM. In the standard game, each element represents one-twelfth of the army, whatever its size; but larger numbers of elements are used in the Big Battle and Giant Battle rule variants. Although each element base is depicted as a rigid rectangular block, this does not imply that the troops it represents are necessarily in such a block or do not vary their position.

Ground Scale and Distance Measurement.

The unit of measurement is the width of an element base (a BW). For movement or maximum shooting range, this is roughly equivalent to 80 paces in real life. Distances are specified in the rules as multiples or halves of a base width. They can be measured on the table either with a selection of rods cut to length, or a with a strip of card or similar material 5 BW long marked at 1 BW intervals, which can also have other information on its reverse to serve as the equivalent of a reminder sheet. You will find that distances can often be estimated visually without measurement. A rectangle 1 BW x ½ BW with a vertical handle is also very useful for measuring gaps. "Within" means "at or closer than".

Time Scale.

Play is in alternate bounds, simulating action and response. The real life time represented varies, since sometimes response was immediate, but sometimes both armies paused for reorganisation or rest. Averaged over the battle each bound represents about 15 minutes. Move distances were those needed rather than the maximum theoretically possible in the time.

Dice.

Each player uses a single ordinary 1 to 6 dice[1], which should be used for the whole game for all purposes, unless changed at the request of the opponent. Dice with spots are more easily read across the table by an opponent than those with numbers.

---

[1]The Oxford English Dictionary gives "dice" as singular and "dice" as plural, with a note that "die" is sometimes used as an archaic alternative form for the singular. The entry for "die" has several meanings, but no reference to "dice". Comparison with "mice", "mouse" and "lice", "louse" suggests that there ought to be a singular form "douse" to go with the plural "dice". I have never met this, so I will not use it but will continue to use "one dice, many dice".

5.4 Troop Definitions.

Troops are defined by battlefield behaviour instead of the usual formation, armour, weapons and morale classes. We distinguish only between troops whose fighting style differs sufficiently to need to be treated differently by either their general or their foe. Apparent anomalies caused by grouping together disparate troops can be rationalised since the disparity is compensated by other factors, such as ferocity or skill. These apparent anomalies are unobtrusive if the army fights opponents of its own era, and are minimised by further defining foot as either "Fast" or "Solid".

Mounted troop types are: Elephants, Knights, Cavalry, Light Horse, Scythed Chariots or Camelry.

Foot troop types are: Spears, Pikes, Blades, Auxilia, Bows, Psiloi, Warband, Hordes, Artillery or War Wagons.

Camp followers and city denizens are not included in the allowed total of 12 troop elements, but are extra elements of armed civilians of no specific troop type, but which if they sally count as "Solid" foot for movement and "Fast" foot for combat.

A few army lists permit some elements defined above as mounted to "dismount" i.e. be exchanged for a foot element, but these cannot later remount. Those listed as / or // can be deployed as either the mounted type or already dismounted as the foot type; those listed as // can also dismount during the game as a complete single element tactical move.

A very few armies have mounted infantry (prefixed by "Mtd"). These are on larger bases with their mounts, but remain foot and differ in that in good going they have the same tactical move as knights and can move more than once per bound.

ELEPHANTS (El), of any breed or crew complement. These were used to charge massed foot, or to block mounted troops, whose frightened horses would often not close with them. Pikes fought them on nearly level terms, and they could be killed by artillery or showers of lighter missiles, or be distracted by psiloi. Maddened by combat, they would always pursue

KNIGHTS, representing all those horsemen that charged at first instance without shooting, with the intention of breaking through and destroying enemy as much by weight and impetus as by their weapons; such as Macedonian companions, Sarmatians, Gothic horse, Norman or medieval knights, with 3 figures to a base (3Kn), Parthian and similar cataphracts in full armour on fully armoured horses trotting in tight formation, with 4 figures to a base (4Kn), and also un-scythed heavy chariots (HCh) with more than 2 animals (unless Libyans) or wheels or crew greater than 2 or armed with a lance.

Massed bows could shoot them down as at Crecy, or steady spears or pikes stop them with a dense array of shields or weapon points, or sword or axemen kill horses in a standing mêlée. Other foot were likely to be ridden down. Knights could be confident of defeating ordinary heavy cavalry, but light skirmishing horsemen were a greater danger. These must sooner or later be charged rather than accept a constant drain of casualties. However, an over-rash pursuit risked being surrounded and shot down in detail. Knights were not well suited to dodging elephants or scythed chariots. A few armies such as Later Byzantines and the Teutonic Order used knights in deep wedges with the most heavily armoured in front and on the sides and lesser troops inside. These are depicted as double elements (6Kn) with figures based in two rows.

CAVALRY, representing the majority of ancient horsemen, primarily armed with javelins, bows or other missile weapons but combining these with sword or lance (Cv), and also light chariots (LCh) with 2 (or if Libyan 4) animals and 1-2 crew. They usually started combat with close range shooting, using rapid archery or circulating formations to concentrate a mass of missiles, but charged when that would serve better or to follow up an advantage. They could destroy or drive away psiloi or auxilia, ride down foot bows caught at a

disadvantage, and force other foot to retire or even destroy them. Not as committed to the charge as knights, they could retire out of range of archery or to breathe their horses between missile attacks on pikes or spears. They were outmatched in hand-to-hand combat by knights, but, being more agile and having missile weapons, were in less danger from light horse, elephants or scythed chariots. A few armies such as the Byzantines used deep formations depicted as double elements (6Cv) with lancers in front and archers behind.

LIGHT HORSE, including all light horsemen (LH) or camel riders (LCm) who skirmished in dispersed swarms with javelin, bow or crossbow and would not charge unshaken enemy; such as Numidians, Huns, Parthian horse archers, Late Roman "Illyrians" or Equites Sagittarii, genitors or border staves. They typically fought by sending a constant  stream of small parties to gallop past shooting several times at close range, then return to rest or change ponies while others took their turn. The boldness engendered by their near invulnerability, the point-blank range and their continuous rapid shooting made them as effective against most foot as much larger numbers of foot archers and more so than cavalry in formation and lacking their large numbers of spare mounts. They did not charge until fatigue, casualties or disorder made the enemy incapable of resisting. If charged, they evaded shooting behind them, ready to turn on an over-confident pursuer. They detested foot archers, who outshot and outranged them, and artillery, who made their rally position unsafe. They were unlikely to destroy solid foot with good shields and/or armour unless these had an open flank, but could greatly hamper their movements. They were often used for wide flanking movements behind the enemy, operating semi-autonomously rather than under close control, so are permitted extra movement out of contact and are rarely affected by distance from the general. Armies with very large numbers of horse archers could form up very deep, increasing the frequency of exchange and the effect of shooting effect; but on a dusty confused battlefield this could make evading a charge risky.

SCYTHED CHARIOTS (SCh), with four horses and usually a single crewman, so with a high power/weight ratio, which, with no need to conserve the horses' energy, enabled them to charge straight ahead at a mad gallop into enemy formations early in a battle to disrupt or destroy them. Since they were usually wrecked in the process, the drivers often jumped out at the last moment, offering some hope to the target that the horses might swerve away from contact. They were mainly dangerous to those troops who offered a solid target and could not dodge easily, so were often countered by psiloi.

CAMELRY (Cm), including those camel-mounted warriors who charged to close quarters or used mass archery, but not those that only skirmished or infantry transported by camel. Their chief value was to disorder those mounted troops that depended on a charge into contact. They were vulnerable to missiles and to troops closing on foot.

SPEARS (Sp), representing all close formation infantry fighting with spears in a rigid shield wall; such as hoplites, Punic African foot, Byzantine skutatoi or Saxon fyrd. The mutual protection provided by their big shields, tight formation and row of spear points

gave them great resisting power, so that two opposed bodies of spears might fence and shove for some time before one broke. Theban hoplites that formed very deep are depicted by double elements (8Sp). Steady spears could usually hold off horsemen, but psiloi or light skirmishing horse could force them to halt and present shields, and might surround and destroy an outflanked body. They are all classed as "Solid".

PIKES (Pk), including all close formation infantry who fought collectively with pikes or long spears wielded in both hands; such as Macedonians, Scots, Flemings or Swiss. Their longer weapons made pikemen even better than spearmen at holding off charging mounted troops. When fighting against foot, the combination of longer weapons and deep formations enabled them to roll over most opponents if they could keep moving forward; though the long shafts also made formation keeping more difficult, so that gaps resulting from terrain or

the stress of combat could be exploited by blades or warband. Any prolonged lack of movement exposed them to flank attacks. Less effective shields made them more vulnerable than spears to bows and psiloi. They are all classed as "Solid", except for irregular

hillmen with long spears used in both hands and mostly lacking shields (3Pk), such as Hittites, Koreans or North Welsh which are classed as "Fast".

BLADES (Bd), including all those close fighting infantry primarily skilled in fencing individually with swords or heavier cutting or cut and thrust weapons; such as Roman legionaries, huscarls, gallo-glaich, dismounted knights, halberdiers, billmen, clubmen or later samurai. They often had

better armour or shields than other foot, weapons that could more readily defeat armour, and often added supplementary missile weapons or closed quickly to avoid missiles. They were less safe than spears or pikes against charging mounted troops, but were superior in hand-to-hand combat to any foot except pikes in deep formations. Blades are classed as "Solid", except for those more lightly equipped but faster moving (3Bd), such as Dacian falx-men, Roman lanciarii or medieval Indian swordsmen, who are classed as "Fast", as are also Swiss halberdiers acting offensively in columns (6Bd), but not dismounted knights mounted 3 to a base to match mounted numbers. Generals operating from stationary command positions accompanied by staff and bodyguards (CP), or carried in litters surrounded by bodyguards (Lit), and standard-bearing command wagons with guards (CWg) of the Khazars and Italian city states are treated as "Solid" Blades except that they cannot move into contact with enemy.

AUXILIA (Ax), representing javelin-armed foot able to fight hand-to-hand but emphasising agility and flexibility rather than cohesion. Irregulars (often mountain peoples) such as Thracians, Armenians and Irish kerns are usually (3Ax) classed as "Fast" They were over-matched in open country by other close fighting foot and more vulnerable to cavalry than Spears, but useful to chase off or support psiloi, to take or hold difficult terrain, as a link between heavier foot and mounted troops or occasionally as a mobile reserve. Those that acquired better weapons or regular discipline such as Hellenistic thureophoroi, Iberian scutarii and Imperial Roman auxilia become (4Ax) classed as "Solid" and can counter Warband.

PSILOI (Ps), including all dispersed skirmishers on foot with javelin, sling, staff sling, bow, crossbow or hand gun. These fought in a loose swarm hanging around enemy foot, pestering it with a constant dribble of aimed missiles at close range and running out of reach if charged. They rarely caused serious casualties, but were very useful to slow and hamper enemy movements,

to protect the flanks of other troops, to seize, hold or dispute difficult terrain, to co-operate with cavalry, and to counter elephants or scythed chariots. Unsupported psiloi in the open were vulnerable to cavalry. Archers integral to units of close fighting foot are not classed as psiloi, but assumed to be included in their elements. Psiloi are all classed as "Fast".

BOWS (Bw, Lb or Cb), representing foot formed in bodies who shot at longer range than psiloi, often in volleys at command. Weapons that often penetrated armour at very short range, such as longbows (Lb) or crossbows (Cb), are differentiated by effect. Troops unhappy to stay and fight hand-to-hand (3Bw, 3Lb, 3Cb) are classed as "Fast",

those that defended themselves with light spears, heavy swords or clubs and sometimes behind stakes or pavises (4Bw, 4Lb, 4Cb) are classed as "Solid"; as also are mixed units with several ranks of close-fighters (rather than a single rank of pavisiers) in front of the shooters and depicted as double elements (8Bw, 8Lb, 8Cb) with close fighter figures in front and bowmen behind.

WARBAND (Wb), including all wild irregular foot that relied more on a ferocious impetuous charge than on mutual cohesion, individual skills or missiles; such as most Celts and Germans. Enemy foot that failed to withstand their impact were swept away, but they were sensitive to

harassment by psiloi and to mounted attack. Those that charged most impetuously, moved most swiftly, were used to woods, but were brittle in defeat (3Wb), such as Britons or Galwegians are classed as "Fast". Those that kept a shield wall in adversity and fought it out toe-to-toe (4Wb) are classed as "Solid".

HORDES (Hd), representing unskilled and unenthusiastic foot levied from peasantry to bulk out numbers and perform the menial work of sieges and camps and typically huddling in dense masses whose inertia provides a kind of staying power allowing them to be classed as "Solid", if only by comparison (7Hd). Others (5Hd) such as rioters, street gangs, revolutionary mobs, religious fanatics and Aztec militia were more enthusiastic, so "Fast" but equally incompetent.

ARTILLERY (Art), whether tension, torsion, counterweight or gunpowder. This could annoy the enemy at long range, destroy war wagons or elephants and counter enemy artillery, but was relatively immobile once deployed, so is "Solid" foot.

WAR WAGONS (WWg), including Hussite mantleted wagons, mobile towers, and other wagons that fought mainly by shooting and could move during battle, but not laagered transport wagons. They are "Solid" because, except for mobile towers which can assault a city, fort or camp, they had great resisting power to blunt attack, but could not themselves charge. They were vulnerable to artillery. Since they could fight all-round, they count the first edge in contact as their front edge when in close combat (but not for moving along a road) and can choose any one edge each bound to shoot from. They could not shoot effectively on the move. In *DBA* they are usually depicted without draft animals, simulating the removal of these before combat, and so can be on square bases.

5.5 Basing your Figures and Models.

All figures must be combined into elements of several figures, or an elephant, vehicle or artillery model, fixed to a thin rectangular base. Base width is critical and must not be changed. It is 60mm for the larger scale and 40mm for the smaller . Players should keep as closely as possible to the minimum depths recommended below. Larger alternatives are to accommodate figures based for other rule sets or over-large figures.

Troop Type		DBA List Code	Base depths in mm for:		Figures or models per base
			Larger scale	Smaller scale	
ELEPHANTS		El	80	40	1 model
KNIGHTS		3Kn	40-45 (60*)	30 (40*)	3
		4Kn	40-45	30	4
		6Kn	80	60	6
		HCh	60 or 80	40	1 model
CAVALRY		Cv	40-45	30	3
		6Cv	80	60	6
		LCh	60 or 80	40	1 model
LIGHT HORSE		LH	40-45	30	2
		LCm	40-45	30	2
SCYTHED CHARIOTS		SCh	60 or 80	40	1 model
CAMELRY		Cm	40-45	30	3
MOUNTED INFANTRY		Mtd-X	60-80	40-60	3-4 + mount
SPEARS	All "Solid"	Sp	20-30	15-20	4
		8Sp	40	30	8
PIKES	"Solid"	4Pk	20-30	15-20	4
	"Fast"	3Pk	30	20	3
BLADES	"Solid"	4Bd	20-30	15-20	4**
	"Fast"	3Bd	30	20	3
	"Fast"	6Bd	60	40	6
AUXILIA	"Solid"	4Ax	30	20	4
	"Fast"	3Ax	30	20	3
BOWS	"Solid"	4Bw, Cb, Lb	30	20	4
	"Fast"	3Bw, Cb, Lb	30	20	3

Troop Type		DBA List Code	Base depths: Larger Scale	Base depths: Smaller Scale	Figures or models per base
BOWS	"Solid"	8Bw, Cb, Lb	60	40	8
PSILOI	All "Fast"	Ps	30	20	2
WARBAND	"Solid"	4Wb	20-30	15-20	4
	"Fast"	3Wb	30	20	3
HORDES	"Solid"	7Hd	40-60	30-40	7-8
	"Fast"	5Hd	40-60	30-40	5-6
ARTILLERY		Art	80	40	1 model
WAR WAGONS		WWg	60 or 120	40 or 80	1 model
GENERAL		CP, Lit or CWg	60 or 120	40 or 80	5-6
Sallying denizens or camp followers			30	20	2-4

* Macedonian companions and some Skythian nobles can be on a deeper base with the centre figure further forward representing an historical wedge formation.

** Knights that have dismounted as blades can be based with 3 figures as when mounted.

Where more than one basing option exists, this usually differentiates troops of the same type who fought slightly differently, such as those classed as "Fast" or "Solid" and/or those who used unusually deep formations. It also helps identify troops of different origins, which can be further distinguished by aligning figures representing regular troops evenly in a single level row, and using a mix of figures of differing type, pose and/or colour scheme placed more randomly for irregulars.

The general's element must be recognisable by his figure, standard or conventional white charger, or rarely by being in a litter (Lit) or command wagon (CWg) or in a temporarily halted command position with staff and guards (CP).

Mounted Infantry are based as 3-4 foot figures plus a vehicle, led mount or mounted figure.

Depict camp followers and city denizens that sally outside their defences as armed civilians.

Double elements required by army lists are based in two rows.

6Kn can have a row of 2 followed by a row of 4, or 3 interleaved ranks of 1, 2 and 3, with the centre 2 of the back row being the lighter type.

6Cv and 6Bd have two rows of 3.

8Sp have 2 ranks of 4.

8Bw have a row of 4 with pavise or shield plus spear followed by 4 with bow or crossbow.

A double element is 1 element of the army's 12, but may count as 2 elements when lost. In partial compensation, it fights in close combat against most foot as if the rear element was providing rear support.

If your army is of individual 6mm figures, use twice as many figures and models as specified above.

Basing of 6mm or 2mm blocks is complicated by them being cast with varying frontages. They must be cut and combined to look realistic, with irregulars and skirmishers often in small random groups.

Use open formation blocks for light horse or psiloi, loose for most knights, cavalry, auxilia, bowmen or warband, and close for cataphracts, spears, pikes and most blades.

5.6 Battlefield Terrain.

Players must be able to provide a battlefield in case they become the defender. As generalship is definable as the skill with which generals adapt their troops' movements to those of the enemy and to the battlefield, varied and realistic terrain is essential for interesting battles. Since so little time is needed to paint *DBA* armies and the playing area is so small, players should invest time and ingenuity in making their terrain as visually attractive as their troops.

Unless a competition organiser provides pre-set terrain, the battlefield is produced by the defending player placing separate terrain features on a flat board or cloth representing flat GOOD GOING such as pasture, open fields, steppe grassland or smooth desert. The defender bisects the battlefield twice at right angles to its edge to produce 4 equal quarters and numbers these 1-4 clockwise from the left.

Choosing and Placing Features.

The types of feature that can be used depend on those of the terrain in which the defending army historically normally fought at home. The defending player chooses and places 1-2 compulsory and 2-3 optional features from those permitted.

Those chosen must include BAD or ROUGH GOING (as defined below) or a River or Waterway, and cannot include more than 1 each of Waterway, River, Oasis, Gully or BUA, or 2 roads, or 3 each of any other feature type. Waterways must be placed first, then compulsory features, then others.

Each feature is diced for:
   A score of 1 to 4 directs that it must be placed within that quarter.
   A score of 5 directs that the quarter is chosen by the defender.
   A score of 6 directs that the quarter is chosen by the invader.

Area features other than Plough or Gentle Hills must be placed entirely within that quarter. A lesser part of any Gentle Hill may, and all Plough and linear features must, extend into 1 only adjacent quarter.

A feature that cannot be placed is discarded.

There must be a gap of at least 1 BW between area features and between an area feature other than a BUA and any battlefield edge.

If terrain is	Compulsory features are :	Optional features are :
ARABLE	1 BUA or 2 Plough.	River, Difficult Hills, Gentle Hills, Woods, extra Plough, Enclosures, Road, Waterway, Scrub, Boggy.
FOREST	1-2 Woods.	River, Marsh, Gentle Hills, extra Woods, BUA.
HILLY	1-2 Difficult Hills.	River, Woods, BUA, Road, extra Difficult Hills.
STEPPE	1-2 Gentle Hills.	River, Rocky, Scrub, 1 only Gully, BUA.
DRY	1-2 Rocky or Scrub	Dunes, Difficult Hills, Oasis, BUA
TROPICAL	1-2 Woods.	River, Marsh, 1 only Gully, BUA, Enclosures, Road, extra Woods.
LITTORAL	1 Waterway	Either Difficult Hills or Marsh, either Woods or Dunes, BUA, Road, River.

AREA TERRAIN FEATURES include those listed below as BAD, ROUGH or GOOD GOING and also BUA.

Each must fit into a rectangle of which the length plus the width totals no more than 9 BW. Only 1 feature can have a length (maximum dimension) of less than 3 BW. Every feature must have both a length and a width (maximum dimension at a right angle to its length) of at least 1 BW.

A Gully's length must be at least 3 times its width. The length of other features must not exceed twice their width. BUA and Plough can have straight edges; otherwise all features must be a natural shape with curved edges. A city or fort can be combined as 1 feature with a larger hill that is also permitted.

Difficult (steep and/or rocky, thickly scrubbed or wooded) Hills, Woods, Marsh and Gully are BAD GOING, which slows the movement of, and is an adverse close combat tactical factor for, some foot and all mounted and may hinder shooting. Dunes and Oases are BAD GOING except to elements of any type with camels.

Rocky, Scrubby or Boggy flat ground, Enclosures (fields subdivided by stone walls, hedges, ditches or in Asia by paddy bunds) are ROUGH GOING, which reduces move distances but is not a tactical factor and does not affect shooting.

Gentle Hills and playing surface other than terrain features are GOOD GOING.

Plough is GOOD GOING but changes to ROUGH GOING if the game's first PIP score is 1, due to heavy rain or crops. An element only partly in GOOD GOING is treated as in the other going. All hills slope up to a centre line crest and give a close combat advantage if part of an element's front edge is upslope of all of its opponent.

LINEAR TERRAIN FEATURES include Waterways, Rivers and Roads.

A **Waterway** represents the sea, a lake edge or a river too wide and deep to be fordable and is impassable. It extends 1-4 BW inwards from an entire battlefield edge and half its length must extend no more than 3 BW in from that edge. It can be bordered by a beach or flood plain extending up to 2 BW further, which is GOOD GOING.

A **River** must run from one battlefield edge to a different battlefield edge or join a waterway. It cannot be wider than 1 BW or longer than 1½ times the distance between its ends. It can cross any feature except a Hill, Dunes, Oasis or BUA. It cannot start or go within 4 BW of any battlefield edge except the 2 edges it flows from and towards. A river can only be entered when attempting to cross it. For movement, a river is neither good nor other going; instead the elements crossing it are restricted by conditions that are constant along its whole length and for the whole game. These restrictions are discovered when the first attempt is made by any player to cross it off-road. An element is defending the bank if it is entirely on land and its close combat opponent is at least partly in the water.

Roads can be paved or be earth tracks (best depicted as pale brown) created by frequent civilian traffic. They are depicted as less than a BW wide, elements moving along them with the centre of their front approximately in the middle of the road, rather than being confined between the road edges. A road must run from one battlefield edge towards the opposite battlefield edge, bending only minimally if desired to avoid terrain features. It cannot begin or end at a waterway edge, but crosses rivers by ford or bridge. It can end at a BUA on a waterway edge. It can only cross a city from city gate to city gate. A second road must cross or join the first. Movement by an element or group in column entirely along a road is in GOOD GOING and counts as straight ahead even when the road curves. Combat on it is in the going it is passing through.

BUILT-UP AREA (BUA)

If a BUA is chosen, it must be a city, fort, hamlet or edifice and will belong to the defender. These are placed like other area features, except that all of a city or fort must be within 6BW of each of 2 battlefield edges and can be on a hill.

At the start of the game a city can and a fort must be garrisoned by one (non-allied) foot element, placed near its centre but representing defenders manning its perimeter. If the garrison is Artillery, its shooting effect is reduced because the artillery is distributed around the perimeter. Thereafter, any single foot element (except War Wagons) can move completely within an undefended city or fort and then garrison it. A garrison or other occupying element does not pursue defeated attackers as the result of an outcome move. Occupiers of a BUA beside any but a paltry river count as defending the bank against enemy elements assaulting it and still partly in that river. A city or fort on a hill includes the hill in its tactical factor so occupiers do not count as uphill nor do assaulters count as being in bad going. Such a city must incorporate an extra road (not counting as a separate terrain feature) from each gate to the nearest hill edge.

(a) **A CITY** has defensive walls, high economic and prestige value and a large population of denizens who will defend it if it has no garrison. It must be modelled with 1 or 2 gates, through which all elements entering or leaving must pass unless they are enemy assaulting it. A single friendly group or element can move through a city, even if it is garrisoned, by using 1 PIP per element to get from just outside the near gate to having the last element moving just outside the far gate.

Denizens of a city are armed civilians initially loyal to the defender, they are not a garrison. If a garrison vacates the city, the denizens continue to defend it. If the garrison is destroyed, they do not. When a garrison or denizens are destroyed in close combat, any one assaulting enemy element (except elephants or a mobile tower) occupies the city and sacks it until its player has a PIP score of 5 or 6. The sacking element can then either garrison the city if eligible to do so, or vacate it. Prior to that, the sacking element does not get a garrison tactical factor in close combat and cannot shoot or be shot at.

Denizens sometimes sallied out to assist a relieving army, so this is allowed if the city does not contain a troop element and there are both enemy and friendly troop elements within 2 BW of the city.

The denizens cannot themselves go more than 3 BW from it. Their fighting value in the open is minimal and the city is undefended in their absence. If the denizens of a city sally out or are destroyed and it is left unoccupied by the enemy or vacated, either side can move into or through it without combat.

If denizens defending inside a city are destroyed by artillery the city surrenders and is not sacked. An appropriate enemy element immediately becomes a garrison on moving into it. If it is not occupied by the enemy or it is vacated; a puppet administration has been put in power and its denizens will defend the city for the enemy. Denizens of a surrendered city cannot sally, as the puppet administration is fully occupied holding down a doubtful populace.

If a city has surrendered during the game and there is no enemy troop garrison or this has been destroyed by shooting, the player that originally owned the city can pay 5 PIPs at the start of any of its side's bounds for its denizens to revolt against and overthrow the puppet administration, resume their original loyalty and defend the city (treachery by an internal faction was the most common reason for a city's fall).

(b) **A FORT** (or castle) has permanent defences and a gate and must start the game garrisoned by a foot element. It has no economic value or denizens. It is left undefended if its garrison vacates it or is destroyed; and can then be moved into and garrisoned by any foot element (except War Wagons) of either side.

(c) **A HAMLET** (or township) is either a small inhabited area of scattered or grouped houses among small enclosed fields, or a larger village or town with denser housing, but no perimeter defences except fences to keep out animals. It has insignificant economic or defensive value and its inhabitants flee when troops approach. It functions only as ROUGH GOING.

(d) **An EDIFICE** is an isolated large building, such as an Amerindian or other pyramid, a pharos, a monastery, a temple or ruins. It has no economic value, denizens or defensive value. It is treated only as BAD GOING, except when it is used as a CAMP.

CAMPS

The camp is the logistical component of the army. It is optional if the army has a city or more than 2 War Wagons, compulsory if it does not.

It must be in GOOD GOING (except Plough) on the rear edge of its side's deployment area or on a waterway or beach, and should have only temporary structures, except that an EDIFICE so positioned can be declared and act as a camp.

A camp must be at least 1 BW x ½ BW and fit into a rectangle the length plus width of which totals no more than 4 BW.

Unless based on an edifice, a camp is depicted as an open space surrounded by an outer perimeter of simple earthwork and/or palisade, laagered wagons, a brush boma, a group of medieval tents with interlaced guy ropes, yurts with tethered ponies, kneeling camels or anything else appropriate to the army.

At the start of the game a camp can be occupied by either

(a) 1 only non-allied troop element (except Elephants or Scythed chariots), which can subsequently vacate it and may be replaced by another such element, or

(b) camp followers (represented either by a camp follower element that can move out of it but without being able to return, or fixed figures that cannot move out of it, but not both).

If neither has been provided, it has been left undefended. A camp that has been entered by any enemy element either as a tactical or outcome move is immediately sacked and ceases to have any defensive or other value.

There are rare historical examples of camp followers leaving the camp to fight in the open but more realistically as a decoy or false reinforcement. This is therefore permitted, but will be of minimal combat value and leaves the camp undefended.

5.7 Fighting the Battle.

Deployment.

Each side dices and adds the aggression factor of its army list to the score, dicing again if the scores are equal. The side with the lower total is the defender, the other is the invader.

The defender chooses and places terrain allowed to its army to create the battlefield.

The invader then selects a base edge.

The defender's base edge is that opposite the invader's edge. If a road crosses the battlefield, one of the intersected sides must be chosen, otherwise any edge that is not opposite a waterway.

Next, both sides place their camp, the defender first.

Then the defender deploys its troop elements, one of which (if eligible) may be used to garrison a city or fort.

Then the invader deploys its elements.

All non-garrison troops must deploy at least 3 BW from the battlefield centre line and 1 BW from any enemy city or fort. Cavalry, Light Horse, Camelry, Mounted infantry and Auxilia or Psiloi must deploy at least 2 BW away from battlefield side edges and others at least 4 BW away.

If a waterway has been placed, either side can reserve 2-3 elements (whose army's home terrain is LITTORAL) to be deployed at the start of its first bound (before PIP dicing) as a single group anywhere along the waterway. At least 1 element of the group must touch the waterway. These elements cannot include Elephants, War Wagons or Artillery.

Sequence of Play.

The defender takes first bound, then the two sides alternate bounds. During each player's bound:

(1) The player dices for Player Initiative Points (PIPs) (representing the general's attention and ability to communicate)

(2) The player uses these PIPs to make tactical moves.

(3) Any Artillery, War Wagons or Bows elements of both sides that are eligible to do so, must shoot once each (in case of dispute in the order the moving player decides) and make or inflict outcome moves.

(4) Any elements of both sides whose front edges are in suitable contact with enemy fight in close combat in the order the moving player decides and make or inflict outcome moves.

Player Initiative Point (PIP) Dicing.

The side starts its bound by dicing. The score is the number of PIPs that can be used for tactical moves this bound. Any unused PIPs are lost, not kept for future bounds.

In each bound, the first move of each single element or column uses 0 PIPs if it is entirely by road, moves until it contacts enemy or friends or moves its full tactical move distance, and does not reverse direction. Each other tactical move uses 1 PIP.

Except in the side's first bound, a move that uses a PIP uses up an extra PIP for each of the two following cases that apply:

(a) If the moving element or group includes any Scythed Chariots not moving into contact with enemy, Elephants, Hordes, War Wagons, Artillery, denizens or camp followers, or is an element currently garrisoning a city, fort or camp.

(b) If the moving element is not the general's element and either its general's element has been lost or is entirely in a BUA, camp, Wood, Oasis, Marsh or Gully or if the element or group to be moved starts more than command distance from its general.

Command distance is 20 BW if entirely Light Horse. Otherwise, it is 8 BW, but is reduced to 4 BW for troops entirely beyond the crest of any Hill, beyond a BUA or a camp, on a Difficult Hill, or in or beyond a Wood, Oasis or Dunes.

Tactical Moves.

A tactical move is a voluntary move that normally uses up PIPs and happens before shooting and close combat. It can be by a single element or a group of elements, but cannot include any element currently in close combat.

It must not be confused with outcome moves (recoils, flees and pursuits), which are compulsory, do not use up PIPs and follow distant shooting or close combat.

A legal tactical move cannot be taken back once the element has been placed unless the initial position was marked and the opponent consents. Such a marker must be removed before starting to move another element.

A tactical move by a single element can be in any direction, even diagonal or oblique, can pass through any gap its leading (not necessarily its front) edge can fit through and can end facing in any direction.

It cannot be used by an element in close combat, which can break-off only by a recoil or flee outcome move.

An element of Knights, Cavalry, Camelry or Light Horse that uses its move to dismount is exchanged (with its front edge in the same place) for the foot type, then moves in subsequent bounds as that foot. It cannot dismount while in any contact with enemy or in an enemy Threat Zone (TZ).

A group is a contiguous set of elements all facing in the same direction with each in both edge and corner-to-corner contact with another; or in at least corner-to-corner contact if part of a wheeling column. **A column** is a group only 1 element wide.

A group can only move forwards. It moves as if entirely of the slowest type included. Each of its elements must move parallel to or follow the first to move, move the same distance, or wheel forward through the same angles with the group's entire front edge pivoting forward around a front corner. No other changes in frontage, direction or facing can be made, even if within a TZ, except to pivot, wheel and/or slide sideways to line up in an enemy TZ, or to conform in close combat.

Groups are temporary: if the whole of a group cannot move, some of its elements will probably be able to move as a smaller group or as separate single elements. Conversely, a group or single element can move to join other elements and make its next move as a group including these. Allied elements can only make a group move with elements of their contingent.

A group move by road, or across bad (not rough) going must be in or into a column unless entirely by Psiloi. A group move can include reducing frontage to form such a column for this or any other purpose. The leading element moves forward, then others successively join behind it, moving as if by single element moves. No element can end with its front edge further to its original rear. Elements that do not join the tail of the column that bound are no longer part of the same group. Once in the column, each element follows the leading element and wheels at the same places through the same angles.

Tactical Move Distance.

Movement is measured in a straight line, from the starting point of the furthest moving front corner of the single element or group to that corner's final position. Except that if the element is following a road or it deviates to avoid terrain, troops or TZ, the distance is measured along the path travelled. A move can be up to:

4 BW	If Light Horse, Cavalry or Scythed Chariots and only in good going.
3 BW	If Knights, Elephants, Camelry or any mounted infantry and only in good going, or if "Fast" foot in any going.
2 BW	If "Solid" Auxilia or "Solid" Warband in any going, or if other "Solid" foot and only in good going.
1 BW	If any troops other than "Fast" foot, Auxilia or Warband and in bad or rough going for any part of the move (except that Artillery and War Wagons cannot deploy or move at all off-road in bad going).
1 BW	If the front edge of any single element or group is in a non-paltry river for part of the move.

Second or Subsequent Tactical Moves during the same bound.

Some elements or groups that have already moved this bound can make a second or subsequent tactical move if there are enough PIPs and only if this does not start or go within 1 BW of enemy unless while moving along a road and is entirely by:

(a)   Light Horse or mounted infantry, and making a second or third move that is entirely in good going.

(b)   Psiloi making a second move either in their side's first bound of the game, or if every element starts entirely in good going and ends at least partially in bad or rough going.

(c)   Troops moving along a road if making a second or subsequent move.

Crossing a River.

Troops that enter a river must continue crossing at the same angle to its course as they enter, or divert by the minimum necessary to line up in close combat with an enemy element.

The first element to try to cross a river off-road during the game must dice for its state, which then applies along its entire length for both sides for the whole game.

A score of 1 or 2 indicates that the river is paltry, too shallow and easy banked to aid defence and can be passed through as if good going,

A score of 3 or 4 that it slows crossing and its banks aid defence,

A score of 5 or 6 that it slows crossing, its banks aid defence and that only single elements or elements in or forming column can cross it during the game, wider groups stopping at the near bank.

Interpenetrating Troops.

If making a tactical move or fleeing, a mounted element can pass through friendly Psiloi or Psiloi pass through any friends, but in both cases only if there is sufficient clear space beyond and enough move to occupy it; and either

    (a)   it starts at least partly directly in front and ends the move lined-up behind or

    (b)   it starts lined-up behind and ends lined-up in front.

Recoilers can pass through friends facing in exactly the same direction to a clear space immediately behind the first element met, but only if either

    (a)   mounted troops recoiling into any friends except Pikes, Hordes or Elephants,

    (b)   Blades recoiling into Blades or Spears,

    (c)   Pikes or Bows recoiling into Blades, or

    (d)   Psiloi recoiling into any friends except Psiloi.

Since the men represented by an element are not necessarily in a rigid permanent formation, one rear corner may pass through another element or an enemy TZ or a terrain feature while the element's front edge pivots or wheels, rearward men having notionally moved directly to their new positions.

Threat Zone.

The area 1 BW deep in front of any edge of a War Wagon or the front edge of any other type of element, or the area within 1 BW of any point of a camp, city or garrisoned fort is its Threat Zone (TZ).

An element or group which is at least partly within or whose front edge enters an enemy TZ or touches its far edge can move only:

(a) to line up its front edge with one such enemy generating the TZ or

(b) to advance into or towards contact with such an enemy or

(c) if a single element, to move straight back to its own rear for the entire move.

 TZs do not affect outcome moves.

Moving into Contact with Enemy.

The general principle is that troops that would contact in real life do so in the game so that moving a front edge into contact with enemy always results in combat.

At the end of the bound's movement phase the contacting element or at least one element of a contacting group must be lined-up with an enemy element, either;

(a)   in full mutual front edge contact, or
(b)   in full front edge to rear edge contact, or
(c)   in front edge to side edge contact with front corners in contact, or
(d)   with no enemy in contact to its front, but in overlap.

If this is not possible, the move does not happen.

One party moves the minimum distance to so conform. Contactors conform using their tactical move, but an extra sideways slide of up to 1 BW is allowed if this is necessary to conform after contacting an enemy front edge. Elements contacted this bound by enemy or whose front edge is still in contact when combat ends automatically conform if necessary.

A single element contacting a single element conforms to it. A single element or group contacting a group conforms to that group. A single element contacted by a group conforms to it unless itself entirely in bad and/or rough going in which case the group conforms. If conforming to a front edge by contactors is prevented by part-element spacing between enemy or physically blocked by elements, terrain or a table edge, contacted elements or groups must either conform or fight as if in full contact and overlapped. Unless turning to face a flank or rear contact, contacted elements conform at contact.

An element can move into edge contact with an enemy flank edge only if it starts entirely on the opposite side of a line prolonging that edge or if partly on the opposite sides of lines prolonging both flank and rear edges. It can move into contact with an enemy rear edge only if it starts entirely on the far side of a line prolonging that edge.

CP, Lit, CWg, Art or WWg cannot move into any contact with enemy, except that a WWg mobile tower can contact an enemy-held city, fort or camp. Other elements except Scythed Chariots can contact a city, fort or camp with their front edge.

Turning to face a flank or rear contact.

Immediately after the movement phase, elements contacted to flank or rear by an enemy front edge turn to face the first enemy element to contact them unless they are already in full front edge contact with another enemy element or providing rear support.

Any existing contacts are adjusted by moving the elements forward, back or the minimum distance sideways to maintain contact. If an element so contacts the flanks of two enemy elements, both these turn to face it if the first must, the second moving to behind the first.

On the rare occasions that a third element is contacted, it is pushed back to make room for the others to turn. A War Wagons element counts the edge first contacted as its front edge, so does not turn. A second element contacting the same edge is treated as if overlapping the nearest flank. That edge of the War Wagon ceases to be treated as its front edge when the contact ceases.

Distant Shooting.

Only Bows, Artillery and War Wagons can shoot. Maximum range is 5 BW if Artillery and 3 BW if Bows or War Wagons. Measure range between the closest points of the shooting edge and the target edge.

The **Shooting Edge** is either (a) the front edge of a Bows or Artillery element, or (b) any 1 BW portion of the perimeter of a city, fort or camp that is garrisoned by the shooting element or of any edge of War Wagons.

The **Target Edge** is either (a) all of, or any single ½ BW portion of, an element edge or (b) any ½ BW portion of the perimeter of a city, fort or camp. It must be entirely within 1 BW of directly in front of part of the shooting edge. Shooting is blocked if uncrossed lines joining the ends of the shooting and target edges have part of any element between them.

Shooting is not possible if either shooters or target are in close combat or providing rear support, but is possible to or from elements that are overlapping and not in close combat. Targets exposed by outcome moves can be shot at.

Artillery can shoot only (a) in their own bound if they did not move, or (b) to shoot back at enemy artillery shooting at them during the enemy bound. Bows and War Wagons cannot shoot if they have moved more than 1BW this bound.

A hill's crest, a city or fort, or a ½ BW depth of difficult hills, woods, oasis, dunes, hamlet or edifice blocks shooting from and at an element base edge entirely beyond any of these. An element that is at least partly in a river or a marsh cannot shoot. An element entirely in a gully cannot shoot or be shot at.

Bows and War Wagons must shoot at a target in their TZ. If there is none, they must shoot at a target that is shooting at them. If neither, they can choose any eligible target. Artillery can always choose its target in its own bound and can shoot through or over enemy Psiloi.

A second or third element shooting at the same target aids the shooting of the nearest by providing it with a tactical factor instead of being resolved separately. Any more elements shooting at that target this bound have no effect. If a shooter whose target does not shoot back is shot at by a third party, this is resolved first, then it shoots using the same dice score.

Close Combat.

In addition to hand-to-hand fighting, close combat includes all use of missiles by mounted troops or foot skirmishers or during a charge or mêlée. It occurs when an element moves into, or remains in, both front edge and front corner-to-corner contact with an enemy element or at least partial front edge contact with a city, fort or camp.

Combat to both front and to flank and/or rear or when overlapped or overlapping:

When an element is in close combat both to front and to flank or rear or in close combat to its front and overlapped, only it and the enemy element in front fight each other. Others only provide tactical factors. A flank or rear contact on an element providing rear support is treated as if on the supported element. An element not in frontal close combat but in mutual right-to-right or left-to-left front corner contact with any enemy element except Psiloi or Scythed Chariots overlaps this; even if it is exposed by a frontal opponent having recoiled, fled or been destroyed that bound.

Any enemies in any mutual flank edge contact overlap each other whether in close combat or not. An element can overlap 2 enemy elements on opposite flanks. Only 1 overlap or flank contact is counted per flank. An element in good going other than Light Horse or Cavalry and which did not move this bound and has any front corner less than 1 BW from a battlefield edge counts as overlapped on that corner unless this is in contact with a friendly element.

Close combat against a city, fort or camp:

Troops assaulting or defending these use their combat factor against foot and do not count overlaps or flank or rear support. A city, fort or camp can be in contact with the front edges of up to 3 assaulting elements.

The defender fights each assaulting element separately in succession, in each combat counting others still in contact as a tactical factor. Combats cease when the defender is destroyed or all assaulting elements have fought.

Elephants can assault a city or fort only at a gate.

Resolving Shooting or Close Combat.

Whether in contact, shooting or only shot at, each player dices for their element, and adds its combat factor below and any rear support, flank support and tactical factors to the score:

	If against foot:	If against mounted:
ELEPHANTS	5	4
BLADES in close combat	5	3
SPEARS, BLADES if shot at or ARTILLERY unless in a city or fort	4	4
KNIGHTS, SCYTHED CHARIOTS, PIKES or WAR WAGONS	3	4
CAVALRY, CAMELRY or AUXILIA	3	3
WARBAND or HORDES	3	2
BOWS	2	4
ARTILLERY in a city or fort; or LIGHT HORSE or PSILOI	2	2
CAMP FOLLOWERS or CITY DENIZENS	2	0

Rear support factors:

These apply when elements have another friendly element of the same type lined-up directly behind them and facing the same direction, and both are in good going.

Pikes add **+3** and Warband **+1** when in frontal close combat against enemy foot other than Psiloi.

Pikes add **+1** when in frontal close combat against Knights, Elephants or Scythed Chariots.

Light Horse add **+1** when in frontal close combat against any troops.

Double elements (6Kn, 6Cv, 8Sp, 6Bd, 8Bw) not in a city, fort or camp add **+1** when in frontal close combat against enemy foot and the double element is entirely in good going.

Flank support factors:

Some "Solid" elements add **+1** when in frontal close combat in good going against enemy foot if at least one flank edge is in mutual side edge and mutual front corner contact with a friendly element.

Spears add +1 if supported by Spears or "Solid" Blades.

"Solid" Bows add +1 if supported by "Solid" Blades.

"Fast" elements neither give nor receive flank support.

Tactical Factors:

Add to or subtract from scores for each of the following tactical factors that applies:

+4	If garrisoning a city or fort; and either in close combat or being shot at.
+2	If camp followers or other foot defending their camp or denizens their city and either in close combat or shot at.
+1	If the general's element; and either in close combat or being shot at.
+1	If in close combat; and either uphill or defending any but a paltry river's bank off-road.
-1	For each enemy element either overlapping or in front edge and front corner-to-front corner contact with flank or in full front edge contact with rear, or for each second or third enemy element aiding opposing element's shooting, or for each of up to 2 additional enemy elements also still assaulting a city, fort or camp.
-2	If any troops but Auxilia, Bows, Warband or Psiloi and in close combat in bad (not rough) going.

Combat Outcome.

An element whose total is equal to or less than that of its opponent may need to make an immediate outcome move, which depends on its own type and that of the opponent in close combat with its front edge or shooting at it.

An element shooting without being shot at disregards an unfavourable outcome. A supporting element in close combat against an enemy element's flank or rear recoils if the friendly element in combat with that enemy's front recoils, flees or is destroyed.

If its total is equal to that of its opponent:

No effect if attacking or defending a city, fort or camp.

Otherwise:

Scythed Chariots	Destroyed.
Knights or Camelry	Destroyed in close combat by any Blades or any Bows that are Lb or Cb, recoiled in close combat by other "Solid" foot. 4Kn recoiled in close combat by 3Kn. Otherwise no effect.
Other mounted	Recoiled by "Solid" foot in close combat, otherwise no effect.
"Fast" foot	Recoiled by "Solid" foot in close combat with it or shooting at it, otherwise no effect.
"Solid" foot	Destroyed by foot if CP, CWg or Lit & in contact on 2 or more edges by enemy front edges, otherwise no effect.

If its total is less than that of its opponent but more than half:

Destroyed if sacking a city or if defenders of a city, fort or camp or denizens or camp followers that have sallied or mounted infantry in bad going. Recoil if in close combat against defenders of a city, fort or camp. No effect if CP, Lit or CWg.

Otherwise:

Elephants	Destroyed by Psiloi, Auxilia, Light Horse or by Artillery shooting. Flee from Elephants. Otherwise, recoil.
Scythed Chariots	Flee if shot at unless at least partly on their rear edge. If not, destroyed.

Knights	Destroyed by Elephants, Scythed Chariots, Camelry or Light Horse. If not, recoil.
Camelry	Destroyed by Scythed Chariots or if themselves in bad going. Flee from Elephants, If not, recoil.
Cavalry	Flee from Scythed Chariots, or if in bad going. If not, recoil.
Light Horse	Flee from Scythed Chariots, from Artillery shooting, or if in bad going. If not, recoil.
Spears, Pikes or Blades	Destroyed by Knights or Scythed Chariots if in good going or by Warband. If not, recoil.
Auxilia	Destroyed by Knights if in good going. If not, recoil.
Bows	Destroyed by any mounted. If not, recoil.
Psiloi	Destroyed by Knights, Cavalry or Camelry if in going the enemy count as good. If not, recoil.
Warband	Destroyed by Knights or Scythed Chariots if in good going. If not, recoil.
Hordes	Destroyed by Knights or Elephants if in good going, or by Warband. Recoil if shot at. If neither, no effect.
War Wagons	Destroyed by Artillery shooting or by Elephants. If not, no effect.
Artillery	Destroyed.

If its total is half or less than half that of its opponent:

Destroyed if defenders of a city, fort or camp.

Otherwise

Cavalry	Flee from Pikes, Spears or Hordes if in good going, or Artillery in close combat. If not, destroyed.
Light Horse	Destroyed if in bad going, or by any mounted, Artillery shooting, Bows or Psiloi. If not, flee.
Psiloi	Destroyed by Knights, Cavalry, Camelry or Light Horse if in going the enemy count as good, or if in close combat against Auxilia, Bows or Psiloi. Recoil from Elephants or Scythed Chariots. If not, flee.
All others	Destroyed.

Destroyed Elements.

A destroyed element is removed.

This represents an unacceptable number of its men being killed, disabled or made prisoner and the remaining survivors dispersing and quitting the battlefield individually, wagons and artillery having been smashed and abandoned by crews, elephants dead, fleeing in panic or captured, or denizens defending a city abandoning the walls. An element that has an enemy front edge in contact with its side or rear edge is destroyed by recoiling, being pushed back, fleeing or being in a column whose front element is destroyed.

Recoiling or Being pushed back.

This represents troops falling back a short distance under enemy pressure or to make space for friends while continuing to maintain formation and facing.

Recoiling or pushed back elements move straight back without turning. An element with a recoil outcome as a result of shooting which was at least partially at its rear edge turns to face its rear before recoiling. A recoiling foot element always moves its own base depth or ½ BW if this is less than its base depth. A recoiling mounted element can choose either to move 1 BW or to move its own base depth if this is less than 1 BW.

If the recoiling element is Elephants, all friends or enemy met that are not in a BUA or camp are destroyed. Elephants recoiling from close combat against the defenders of a city or fort are destroyed. If 2 Elephant elements meet, both are destroyed. Surviving elephants finish their recoil.

If the recoiling element is not Elephants, friends facing in the same direction can be interpenetrated if allowed. If not, they are pushed back far enough to make room unless they are Elephants or War Wagons. Pushed back elements cannot interpenetrate or push back others.

A recoiling or pushed back element whose rear edge or rear corner meets terrain it cannot enter, a battlefield edge, friends it cannot pass through or push back, enemy or a city, fort or camp ends its move there. An element already in such contact with any of these cannot recoil and is destroyed instead.

Fleeing.

This represents a panic individual rush to the rear.

A fleeing element turns 180 degrees in place; and then moves straight forward without turning for its full tactical move distance for the going it starts in. It then stops until making a tactical move or conforming to further contact by enemy.

If it contacts a side battlefield edge, it pivots and continues the move along that edge towards its rear battlefield edge. If any part of it crosses any other battlefield edge it is removed as lost.

It stops before completing its move and lines up if its front edge (or front corner only) contacts any of:
(a)   enemy (whom it will fight next bound),
(b)   friends it cannot pass through,
(c)   a city, fort or camp,
(d)   a waterway, or
(e)   for troops other than Psiloi or Light Horse, any bad going except marsh it is not already at least partly in.

It is destroyed if it starts with an enemy front edge in contact with its flank or rear edges, or if after turning it cannot move at all, or if it enters any river.

If a friendly or enemy element prevents further movement by fleeing Elephants or Scythed Chariots, both elements are destroyed.

Pursuing.

This represents following up a retiring close combat opponent or panicked survivors of a destroyed element with the intention of continuing to kill them.

An element in a city, fort or camp or in bad going (other than marsh or gully) or whose pursuit move would cross a battlefield edge or enter such bad going, does not pursue.

Otherwise an element whose close combat opponents recoil, flee or are destroyed (and all elements in a column behind such an element) must immediately pursue, but only if:
(a)   The defenders of a city, fort or camp are destroyed in close combat then one assaulting element immediately moves in.
(b)   An element of Knights (other than 4Kn), Scythed Chariots, Elephants or Hordes pursues 1 BW straight ahead.

(c)   An element that is of Pikes, Blades (but not CP, Lit or CWg) or Warband and that fought against any foot except Psiloi pursues ½ BW straight ahead.

If a pursuing element's front edge contacts enemy or its front corner contacts an enemy front edge, they line up immediately as if contact was by a tactical move, but the resulting combat is resolved next bound.

Lost Elements.

An element has been lost if it has been destroyed, or has recoiled, fled or been pushed back across a battlefield edge.

5.8 Winning and Losing the Battle.

The first side that at the end of any bound has now lost a total of 4 elements not including Scythed Chariots, Hordes, camp followers or denizens and has also lost more such elements than the enemy, has lost the battle.

The first double element lost counts as 2 elements lost.

A general lost during the battle counts as 1 extra element lost.

A camp that has been sacked by enemy counts as 1 element lost.

A city occupied by enemy during the battle which has not been re-captured or been subject to a revolt counts as 2 elements lost if it was used without a camp or 1 if used with a camp.

Scythed Chariots do not count towards the lost total because while expensive to provide their loss is expected and discounted.

Hordes do not count because other troops do not regard them as equals or of much importance.

Camp followers and denizens do not count because they are self-replacing (there are usually plenty of hopeful new prospective inhabitants for a once prosperous city and of hungry peasants willing to adopt soldiers who will feed them).

5.9 Extended or Multiple Games.

Multi-Game Tournaments.

Tournaments consist of several rounds of games, each usually played to a time limit, commonly of 60 minutes.

Army composition and allies must be declared by the start of the first game and cannot be changed between games; except that an element listed as / or // can be deployed at the start of each game as either mounted or dismounted.

Organisers of established tournaments usually have their own tried and tested scoring systems. If you are designing your own system, it needs to ensure that a single massive victory does not outweigh a more consistent string of successes, that wins are always more valuable than draws/unfinished games and players are not encouraged to get ahead in a game by a small margin then stall.

A Swiss-chess competition format enables players potentially travelling long distances to play in every round. Anachronistic pairings should be minimised by organisers giving priority to pairings between those armies with equal cumulative scores whose army lists specify each other as historical enemies. This principle can be taken further by each player bringing a historically opposed pair of armies and dicing for which player's pair is used, the other player then choosing which he commands; but at the cost of reducing variety.

If it is important to eliminate draws (as in knock-out competitions) and neither side has achieved victory when the time limit is reached, one possible solution available to the organiser is to eliminate both players.

Big-Battle *DBA*.

This is a variant enabling a single player on each side to use a larger army divided into commands and a larger playing area, but without the increased historical detail of DBMM.

Each army consists of 36 elements. If it is from a single list, multiply the number of elements of each type allowed by the army list by 3. Each of the 3 generals controls a command of at least 6 elements chosen from those available. The army can instead include allied commands of the same year from lists with a different number or with the same number but a different letter, which are always full 12-element independent armies from those lists. Allied elements can only be in an allied command. If there is only 1 allied command, the remainder of the army is then restricted to its list multiplied by 2 instead of 3. If there are 2 allied commands, they must be from different lists and the remaining command is also a normal 12-element army from its own list. One non-allied general must be designated as Commander-in-Chief (C-in-C). The C-in-C and all ally-generals must be of a troop type specified by their list as general. Other generals can be any element of their list except Lit, CWg, CP, Hordes, Scythed Chariots or Artillery, but cannot ride an elephant unless the C-in-C could ride an elephant.

The width of the battlefield is doubled, but the depth remains the same. The number of compulsory features is changed to 1-3 and the number of optional features is changed to 2-4. There still cannot be more than 1 each of Waterway, River, Oasis, Gully or BUA; or more than 2 Roads, or more than 3 features of the same type.

An allied command must be provided with its own camp; otherwise the whole army has 1 normal-size camp unless it has a City and chooses to use this instead. A camp can only be defended by an element of its own command or camp followers.

The defender places terrain as in standard *DBA*, except that a Waterway cannot be placed on a long side. The invader chooses one long side as his base edge, the defender takes that opposite. Either the defender deploys all commands, then the invader deploys all his (the quickest method; and note that the defender has first move); or the defender deploys 1 or more commands, then each in turn places a command. Each element not in a city, fort or camp must be deployed within 8 BW of its command's general. A littoral landing must be by a full command provided by an army whose own home topography is LITTORAL; and all that command's elements must deploy within 1 BW of the Water Way.

One PIP dice is needed for each command. All a side's dice must be the same colour except that an allied command's dice must be a different colour and is always used for that command. The player must write down after terrain has been placed and base edges chosen which non-allied command will always be given the highest scoring dice, which the next highest scoring dice, and which the lowest scoring dice. He discloses this when he first dices for PIPs. Plough is rough if first bound PIPs total less than 8. A command's PIPs cease to be diced for when all its elements have been lost or left the battlefield. Once in each game, the C-in-C's element can add +1 to its combat score after this has been calculated.

An element is lost if it is destroyed or crosses a battlefield edge, but not if only demoralised. The first double element lost by each command counts as 2 elements lost, and the loss of its general as an extra element lost. An allied command whose camp is sacked counts this as extra losses only to that command. Any other camp sacked or city currently controlled by the enemy counts as extra losses to each non-allied command.

A command that at the start of any of its bounds whose lost elements other than Scythed Chariots, Hordes, camp followers or denizens total a third of its original troop elements is permanently demoralised. During the remainder of the game it cannot make tactical moves, but it can use the same number of PIPs as for a move to turn and hold in place individual elements or to hold in place groups. Other elements not in close combat immediately flee directly towards the nearest point on the army's base edge, but making an initial turn if necessary. This is repeated at the start of each subsequent friendly bound, each element not held that bound or in close combat fleeing whether or not it fled before. Elements not in a city, fort or camp suffer a -2 tactical factor in close combat. A command that has lost half of all its original troop elements is removed.

An army whose cumulative total of lost elements at the end of any bound other than Scythed Chariots, camp followers or denizens is at least half its original troop elements or has 2 of its commands removed or demoralised; and that has also lost more such elements in that bound than the enemy has lost the battle.

Giant *DBA*.

Giant *DBA* is an extension of Big Battle *DBA* for games with several players on each side and/or re-fighting large historical battles.

A separate player controls each general (or more than 1 general). Each side's C-in-C must specify either that all generals dice independently for PIPs, or specify the order in which PIP dice are to be allocated among them according to their scores.

Army size is increased to 12 elements x number of generals. The width of the battlefield is increased to 3 times that of standard *DBA* and the depth can optionally be increased by up to half.

The number of compulsory features becomes 1-4 and the number of optional features becomes 3-6, not more than 4 of which can be the same type.

Historical Refights.

As Big Battle *DBA* or Giant *DBA*, except that the armies and terrain are based on those of the large historical battle.

The battlefield area must be scaled to the size of the area historically fought over. Terrain features are not chosen by the usual selection rules, but are chosen and placed by agreement to duplicate the terrain of the real battle

.Research the number of commands and troops actually used, then calculate the number of elements to be used according to the following ratios, representing the number that would occupy the same space as an element at the ground scale used.

An element of mounted or foot warriors represents

500-600 foot other than horde,

1,000+ horde, or

250-300 horse or camel riders.

Other elements each represent up to 25 elephants or 50 chariots, war wagons or artillery pieces.

Chapter Six: A Selection of Army Lists

The full DBA Army Lists comprise over 500 lists covering the entire world for the whole period from 3000 BC to 1520 AD. This chapter contains a selection of historical conflicts, spread over the same period of time and space and includes the lists for those armies involved. These lists have the same reference numbers, so the Marian Roman Army has reference II/49 indicating it is the 49th army in section II of the full lists.

These lists are grouped into conflicts between historical pairs of opponents for a given campaign or important battle. The section for each conflict is self-contained even though this means that a few armies appear twice. Most of the armies included here also fought against other opponents who are not listed here and sooner or later you will need the full DBA Army Lists to give the complete picture. This chapter gives you a starting point and wide choice of pairs of armies, hopefully wide enough that everyone can find some armies he or she will enjoy using.

Troop Definitions and Terminology

An army list is made up of all the different types of elements that can be used by that army, and the numbers of each type available. Each troop entry lists the number of elements of that sort that can be used, the name, and the type code. The meanings of the type code are described in Chapter Five in the section on basing troops.

A single slash between two codes means that either option can be used by all those elements (e.g. 2 x 3/4 Bw can be 2 elements of 3Bw or 2 elements of 4Bw but not one of each). Similarly a single slash between a mounted type and a foot type means that in any game the player can choose to deploy either all mounted or all foot.

Also note that "3 x Sp or 4Wb" means that you have three elements and can have some Sp and some Wb while "3xSp or 3x4Wb" means that all three elements must be the same, but you can choose which type they are.

A double-slash "//" between 2 codes means that an element deployed as mounted can be exchanged for the dismounted element during the game, but cannot then change back.

Psiloi and other foot that are listed as 3, 5 or 6 to a base are classed as "Fast", others as "Solid".

For example, we have:

II/49 Marian Roman Army 105-25 BC: 1 x General (Cv or 4Bd), 1 x Gallic, Spanish, Macedonian, Greek or similar auxiliary cavalry (Cv) or javelin-throwing Numidian, German, Illyrian or similar light horse (LH), 5 x legionaries (4Bd), 2 x legionaries (4Bd) or Spanish, Illyrian or similar auxiliary foot (4Ax) or Syrian horse archers (LH), 1 x German, Numidian, Spanish or similar javelinmen (Ps or 3Ax), 1 x archers or slingers (Ps), 1 x Numidian elephant (El) or wild Gauls (4Wb), cavalry (Cv) or requisitioned city bolt-shooters (Art).

From this we need to choose 12 elements.

1) We must have a General. He may be either an element of Cavalry or an element of legionaries (4 Blades). In Chapter Two, Marcus chose an element of Blades.

2) One element of either Cavalry or Light Horse. Marcus chose an element of German Light Horse.

3) Five elements of Legionaries (4 Blades).

4) Two elements who could be either Legionaries or Auxiliaries of various types or Syrian Horse Archers. Any mixture is allowed. Marcus chose two Legionaries making a total of 8 elements of Blades in his army.

5) One element of Javelinmen, either Psiloi or Auxiliaries. Marcus chose an element of Psiloi.

6) One element of Psiloi, either Archers or Slingers. Marcus chose archers.

7) The final element allows a large choice, it could be either an elephant or Gaulish warband or Cavalry or Artillery. Marcus chose Cavalry.

So this gave his army as listed in Section 2.4.

Home Terrain

This is usually that of the army's heartland, but sometimes that of a border area where the entry of invaders will be opposed.

Aggression Factor

This is a number from 0 to 4, based on how likely the army was historically to fight at home or to invade another nation. Opposing armies each add their aggression factor to the score of a dice, then compare totals to decide which army fights in home terrain, i.e. which is the defender.

Sources

The references included here will give basic information about your chosen army as well as background reading, but they are only a starting point. You will find additional information, both from other books and from online resources and will soon find that the experts disagree among themselves. You will have to use your own judgement to decide which interpretation to follow.

Using a search engine such as Google will lead you to websites such as Wikipedia which are useful for dates, persons and geography. Indeed Wikipedia is an excellent starting place, but don't stop there. Most of the entries have further references and you should read these to get the full picture.

Original sources (often in translation) are very useful if allowance is made for bad translation or not being exactly contemporary. Eyewitness accounts are best.

Historical novels can bring an era to life and many authors are very knowledgeable. For example, Alfred Duggan fought in Norway, rode horses cross-country, was widely travelled in the near east, studied Crusader castles and taught history and classics before he wrote his first novel "*Knight with Armour*" (set in the First Crusade). Another author is Harry Sidebottom, the author of the "Ballista" series (set in the third century AD) who lectures in classical history at the University of Oxford.

Three useful publications for geographical and historical relationships are "*The New Penguin Atlas of Ancient History*" and "*The New Penguin Atlas of Medieval History*" by Colin McEvedy and David Woodroffe and "*The Geographic Background of Greek & Roman History*" by M. Cary.

Last but certainly not least, "*Slingshot*", the journal of the Society of Ancients, often includes articles on obscure armies; and past issues are available to Society members on disc from *www.soa.org.uk*

Conflict 1: Sargon the Great

I first met this period when I visited the British Museum as a teenager and saw the "Standard of Ur" – a mosaic panel showing the troops of the period marching across it which can be seen on the museum's website *https://www.britishmuseum.org* This inspired me to read Sir Leonard Woolley's account of his excavations between 1922 and 1934. The work has continued and current thinking gives a picture of independent cities in the fertile area near the two mighty rivers, the Tigris and the Euphrates. Each city had its own gods, was ruled by an alliance between the priests and priestesses in their temple and the king and was supported by the farmers in the surrounding region. Wars were thought of as struggles between rival cities' gods represented by the cities' armies, but for many years they were evenly matched and no single city gained lasting dominance over the others.

I/1b Early Sumerian Army 2799-2334 BC: 1 x General on foot (4Pk or if Kish 3Bd) or in battle car (HCh) or straddle-car (LCh), 1 x battle car (HCh) or straddle-car (LCh) or archers (4Bw), 6 x spearmen (4Pk), 1 x spearmen (4Pk) or archers (4Bw), 2 x skirmishers with bows, slings or javelins (Ps), 1 x Martu Bedouin (3Ax) or skirmishers (Ps).

Terrain Type: Arable. **Aggression**: 2. **Enemies** include I/1b each other.

The bulk of Sumerian armies were close-order foot with long spears held in both hands and without shields, relying instead on thick capes of leather or felt studded with copper discs. The leather was often dyed red or green and the felt would be buff or off-white.

Four-wheeled battle cars drawn by four asses came into use about 2800 BC and are classed as HCh because of their lack of manoeuvrability. Straddle-cars (like a chariot but with a single rider sitting astride a saddle) were also used. From about 2500 BC, large body shields were carried; either by separate shield-bearers leaving the spearmen's hands free, or by the spearmen themselves. In battle, the spearmen were preceded by unshielded skirmishers using bows, slings or javelins. Household guards of the northern state of Kish used heavy broad-headed axes and so a Kish general's element can be Blade.

The dramatic change came with the career of Sargon the Great (the fabled "Sharru-kin"). Starting from humble origins, he became king of Kish. He built an empire by conquering the other cities near Kish and then extended his empire by conquering the whole of Mesopotamia and founded a new capital at Akkad, near Kish. Later he reformed the army (I/11a) and extended his control over the whole of the Fertile

Crescent from the Persian Gulf to the Mediterranean Sea. His descendants struggled to hold onto his empire, which was racked by massive revolts. However the army and its generals remained loyal and the empire survived as long as they had only one revolt to deal with at a time.

I/11a Akkadian Army 2334-2193 BC: 1 x General (Sargon the Great or one of his descendants) on 4-wheeled battle car (HCh) or platform car (LCh) or on foot (3Bd), 6 x spearmen (3/4Pk), 1 x archers (4Bw), 3 x skirmishing archers or slingers or javelinmen (Ps), 1 x emergency reserve (7Hd) or Guti, Lullubi or Bedouin levies (3Ax).

Terrain Type: Arable. **Aggression**: 4. **Enemies** include I/1c Sumerian Armies & I/11a civil wars among Akkadian armies.

The Sumerian "Great Revolt" against Akkad entered mythology following Naram-Suen's victory in nine epic battles in a single year.

Finally Mesopotamia was over-run by the Guti and Lullubi around 2193 BC when the Akkadian Empire, was not able to withstand multiple revolts at the same time.

I/1c Great Sumerian Revolt Army 2250 BC: 1 x General (Naram Suen) in battle car (HCh) or straddle-car (LCh), 1 x battle car (HCh) or straddle-car (LCh), 4 x spearmen (4Pk), 2 x spearmen (4Pk) or archers (4Bw), 2 x skirmishers with bows, slings or javelins (Ps), 2 x levies and emergency reserves (7Hd) or skirmishers (Ps).

Terrain Type: Arable. **Aggression:** 2. **Enemy**: I/11a Akkadian armies.

References: *Armies of the Ancient Near East* N. Stillman & N. Tallis, *Warfare in the Ancient Near East* W. J. Hamblin, *Ur of the Chaldees* C.L. Wooley, *Cambridge Ancient History* Vol.1 Part 2, British Museum website *https://www.britishmuseum.org*

Conflict 2: The Hyksos in Egypt.

There are several sets of chronologies suggested for Egyptian History but the periods are defined by their dynasties. Thus we have the "Early Dynastic Period" (Dynasties 1-2), the "Old Kingdom" (3-6), the "First Intermediate" (7-10), and the Middle Kingdom (11-12). The Hyksos ruled during the "Second Intermediate Period" (13-17) and were followed by the "New Kingdom" (18-21). The highest and the lowest chronologies differ by about 30 years and those of the Egyptologists Grimal, Baines & Malik are used here.

It is now thought that Dynasty 13 started in control of all Egypt, but ended with their capital at Thebes and only controlling Upper Egypt. They were followed by Dynasty 17.

Dynasties 14 and 16 were based in Memphis and the Nile Delta and consisted of many short-lived Pharaohs. They fought among themselves with armies defined below:

I/2b Early Egyptian Army 1689-1541 BC: 1 x General (LCh), 4 x archers (4Bw), 2 x menfat (3Bd), 1 x javelinmen & quiver-carriers (Ps), 1 x Medjay or Nubians (3Bw or Ps), 2 x conscripts (7Hd), 1 x Bedouin slingers or Libyan javelinmen (Ps).

Terrain Type: Littoral **Aggression:** 1. **Enemies** include I/2b each other and I/17a & I/17b Hyksos armies.

Egyptian armies consisted of a core of hereditary troops who were archers, menfat and specialist skirmishers pairing a javelin thrower and a quiver carrier, supported by provincial conscripts under their local nobles and by foreign mercenaries. Menfat ("shock troops") were close fighters with axe and shield. Archers and close-combat troops usually formed up in separate bodies in the centre of the battle line with the lighter troops on the flanks.

From about 1645 BC, the Hyksos or "rulers of foreign lands" (probably Amorites from Syria) conquered the northern half of Egypt and established a dynasty of six rulers (Dynasty 15). The first one, Sheshy or Salatis became Pharaoh in 1644/5 BC, set up a new capital in Avaris and a new priesthood of the local god Seth.

I/17a Early Hyksos Army 1645-1591 BC: 1 x General in 2-horse 2-crew chariot (LCh), 4 x retainers with sickle-sword or axe plus javelins (3Bd), 1 x javelinmen (4Ax), 3 x Aamu Bedouin warriors (3Ax) or Libyan skirmishers (Ps), 2 x Syrian, Aamu or Libyan skirmishers (Ps),

1 x Egyptian levies (7Hd) or skirmishers (Ps).

Terrain Type: Littoral. **Aggression:** 2. **Enemies** include I/2b Early Egyptian Army and I/17a each other.

Meanwhile in Thebes, the last of Dynasty 16, the Pharoah Kamose, made a serious attempt to remove the Hyksos kings and died in battle as a result. He was succeeded by his brother Ahmose, the first Pharoah of the Dynasty 18, who continued the struggle and succeeded in defeating the Hyksos. He was the first Pharaoh of the New Kingdom. The sixth Hyksos Pharaoh, Khamudy, was driven out by Ahmose around 1537 BC.

I/17b Later Hyksos Army 1590-1537 BC: 1 x General (Khamudy) (LCh), 2 x 2-horse 2-crew chariots (LCh), 3 x retainers (3Bd), 2 x Aamu warriors (3Ax), 1 x Aamu or Libyan warriors (3Ax), 2 x archers or slingers (Ps), 1 x archers (Ps) or levies (7Hd).

Terrain Type: Littoral **Aggression:** 2. **Enemies** include I/2b & I/22a Egyptian Armies.

I/22a New-Kingdom Egyptian Army 1543-1200 BC: 1 x General (Kamose or Ahmose) in 2-horse chariot (LCh), 3 x 2-horse 2-crew chariots (LCh), 3 x spearmen (3Bd), 3 x archers (4Bw), 1 x archers (4Bw) or heavy axe- men (4Bd), 1 x skirmishing archers or javelinmen (Ps).

Terrain Type: Littoral. **Aggression**: 2. **Enemies** include I/17b Later Hyksos Army.

References: *Armies of the Ancient Near East* N. Stillman & N. Tallis, *Warfare in the Ancient Near East* W. J. Hamblin, *Cambridge Ancient History* Vol 1 Part 2, *Warfare in Ancient Egypt* B. McDermott, *Soldiers of the Pharaoh* N. Fields, *The Hyksos Period in Egypt* C. Booth.

Fiction (for background rather than accurate information): *Shadow Hawk* by Andre Norton, *The Right Hand of Amun* and others by Lauren Haney. *Murder in the Place of Anubis* and others by Lynda S. Robinson.

Conflict 3: The Battle of Kadesh (Qadesh) 1274 BC

The battle of Kadesh (Qadesh) was fought between the Hittite King Muwatallis and Pharoah Rameses II of Egypt. Kadesh lies on the boundary between these two empires. Each year the Society of Ancients holds a "Battle Day" featuring an important historical battle and inviting players to demonstrate many different sets of rules and report on how well the different sets may be used to recreate this battle. In 2011 the Battle of Kadesh was chosen and consequently was discussed in Slingshots Numbers *120, 121, 122, 273, 275, 277 & 294.* It was probably the largest chariot battle in recorded history.

Muwatallis became King around 1308 BC and found himself with a troubled kingdom with revolts by the Gasgans in the north and the various tribes in the west. Active campaigning in the early part of his reign enabled him to create his own empire extending as far as Kadesh.

Rameses II wished to be remembered as a mighty warrior who extended the control of the lands subject to Egypt to create an empire and he regarded Kadesh as one of his cities. His reaction to news to the Hittite capture of this city was to summon his armies and set out to recapture it. This resulted in the battle and the armies involved are described below.

I/24b Later Hittite Imperial Army 1274-1180 BC: 1 x General (Muwatallis) in 2-horse 3-crew chariot (HCh), 1 x 2-horse 3-crew chariot (HCh), 2 x 2-horse 2-crew chariots (LCh), 4 x Hittite spearmen (3Pk), 2 x Anatolian or Syrian spearmen (3Ax), 1 x archers or slingers (Ps), 1 x vassals (7Hd or Ps).

Terrain Type: Arable. **Aggression:** 2. **Enemies** include I/22a New Kingdom Egyptian Army.

At the battle of Kadesh, the Hittite heavy 3-man chariots surprised the Egyptian and so were probably a recent innovation, foreshadowing the later replacement by most nations of light chariots by chariots with more horses and larger crew. They are depicted on Rameses II's triumphal reliefs of the battle as manned by shieldless driver, shieldless spearman and shield-bearer. Only the king's chariot is depicted with an archer or quiver, but earlier reliefs show these, so the reason for their absence is probably the routine Egyptian denigration of an opponent, though the use of the spears from chariots does seem to have been emphasised. The army also still had light Syrian and Anatolian chariots. Hittite infantry at Kadesh are depicted in deep rectangular blocks. The teheru (elite troops) depicted with long spears (often used two-handed) and sometimes shields are thought to be Hittites, those with short spear in one hand, sword in the other and no shield to be Syrian.

I/22a New-Kingdom Egyptian Army 1543-1200 BC: 1 x General (Rameses) in 2-horse chariot (LCh), 3 x 2-horse 2-crew chariots (LCh), 3 x spearmen (3Bd), 3 x archers (4Bw), 1 x archers (4Bw) or heavy axe-men (4Bd), 1 x skirmishing archers or javelinmen (Ps).

Terrain Type: Littoral. **Aggression:** 2. **Enemies** include I/24b Hittite Imperial Army.

Egyptian armies consisted of a core of hereditary troops who were archers, menfat and specialist skirmishers pairing a javelin thrower and a quiver carrier, supported by provincial conscripts under their local nobles and by foreign mercenaries. Menfat were close fighters with axe and shield, sometimes including marines or "spearmen of the residence". Archers and close-combat troops usually formed up in separate bodies in the centre of the battle line with the lighter troops on the flanks. Early New-Kingdom infantry are often shown running with an axe in the right hand, a spear in the left and a small shield slung behind one shoulder. New Kingdom armies added massed chariotry to the tactics of the Middle Kingdom armies. Surviving chariots have axle lengths from 1.98 to 2.36m.

The battle of Kadesh produced a stalemate. Both armies suffered many casualties and so when Rameses offered a peace treaty, Muwatallis accepted it. Rameses returned to Egypt to boast of his victory and Muwatallis kept Kadesh for the rest of his life.

References: *Armies of the Ancient Near East* N. Stillman & N. Tallis, *War in Ancient Egypt* A.J Spalinger, *Fighting Pharaohs* R.B Partridge, *Warfare in Ancient Egypt* B. McDermott, *Slingshot 120, 121, 122, 273, 275, 277 & 294, Hittite Warrior* T. Bryce.

Conflict 4: The Trojan War about 1200 BC.

The semi-legendary Trojan War of about 1200 BC described by Homer is now thought to be a heavily-embroidered account of a war between the Achaean Greeks and the city of Troy/Ilium/Ilion which controlled trade access to the Black Sea and to reflect the military practice of this era. Homer's poem should be thought of as an historical novel set in the later years of the ten-year siege by the Achaeans. It was only the first of many such dramatisations throughout the succeeding centuries. Many of the Greek legends, poems and plays featured the heroes of the Trojan War and their adventures before and after the siege of Troy. Later the Romans got in on the act with the story of Aeneas, a refugee from Troy, who fled with his family and eventually settled in Italy where his descendants founded Rome. The story has continued to the present day, with Shakespeare's "Troilus and Cressida" and the many novels, plays and films since then.

With such a vast and colourful array of stories and legends, it becomes very hard to identify the actual history behind them and even harder to decide accurate details of the armies, how they were equipped and how they fought.

The Iliad has vivid accounts of personal combat between individual heroes and it is widely accepted that the Greek armies were unable to enter Troy until they used the subterfuge of the wooden horse to get warriors inside and open the gates.

If you visit the archaeological site at Hisarlik today, you will see an imaginative reconstruction of the wooden horse just inside the gateway. The archaeological site has its own legend, the story of Heinrich Schliemann who read translations of the Iliad as a child and later travelled to Hisarlik, which he identified as the site of Troy, and obtained permission to excavate there. Although he failed to identify the correct levels of the city described in the Iliad, he did find the correct site and the cache of golden jewels, which he called the "Jewels of Helen", have become as potent a legend as the original poem.

Ilium is taken to be the "Wilusa" of the Hittite records and an account of Hittite king Tudhaliya IV sending a Hittite army to aid Wilusa against an attack by Attarsiyas ruler of the Ahhiiyawa may refer to the same war.

Homer described the spearmen as pressing "shield against shield in their closed formation, bristling with shields and spears". Since his epic was composed much later, some of his graphic descriptions may be coloured by contemporary practise, and in particular, charioteers dismounting to fight may be an anachronism.

Where his charioteers do fight mounted, they sometimes thrust with spears, but usually throw javelins. In the Iliad, the Myrmidons are the ferocious but undisciplined followers of Achilles. The Pylians commanded by the arch-conservative Nestor are assumed here to use the old figure-of-eight shields and two-handed long spears.

I/26a Achaian Army: 1 x General (in chariot (LCh//4Bd), 3 x heroic charioteers (LCh//4Bd), 4 x spearmen (Sp), 2 x spearmen (Sp) or Pylians (4Pk), 1 x Myrmidons (4Wb) or javelinmen (Ps), 1 x javelinmen, archers or slingers (Ps).

Terrain Type: Littoral. **Aggression:** 3. **Enemies** include I/26a (each other) as well as I/26b the Trojans.

I/26b Trojan Army: 1 x General in chariot (LCh//4Bd), 3 x heroic charioteers (LCh//4Bd), 4 x spearmen (Sp), 1 x spearmen (Sp) or Lukka (3Bd), 1 x archers (3Bw or Ps), 2 x javelinmen, archers or slingers (Ps).

Terrain Type: Littoral. **Aggression:** 1. **Enemies** include I/26a the Achaians.

References: *Armies of the Ancient Near East* N. Stillman & N. Tallis, *Early Greek Warfare* P.A.L Greenhalgh, *The Iliad* Homer, *The Legend of Odysseus* P. Connolly, *The Attack on Troy* R. Castleden, *Schliemann's Discoveries of the Ancient World* C. Schuchhardt. *The King in Splendour* G. Shipway (novel).

This is still a popular topic and new books and films appear all the time. The Wikipedia entry for "Helen of Troy" has a long list of references.

Conflict 5: The Hebrew conquest of the "Promised Land"

Many of you will have met this at school as I did. The Bible contains the account of how plucky little Israel was led out of slavery in Egypt by Moses, who died at the end of the trek across the desert. After this Joshua led them into the "Promised Land" and they conquered the local inhabitants (the Canaanites) to take possession of the home promised by their God. The Canaanite list covers the city-states of Canaan and Syria after the fall of the Amorite dynasties to the Hittites and describes the armies fielded by Jericho and others during the Hebrew advance.

I/20b Canaanite Armies 1595 -1100 BC: 1 x General in 2-horse 2-crew chariot (LCh), 3 x Maryannu 2-horse 2-crew chariots (LCh), 1 x royal guard (4Bw or 3Bd), 2 x Hupshu spearmen (3Ax), 2 x Khepetj or 'Apiru spearmen (3Ax or 7Hd), 2 x Hupshu, Khepetj or Apiru archers (Ps), 1 x Bedouin javelinmen, archers or slingers (Ps).

Terrain Type: Arable. **Aggression:** 2. **Enemies** include I/27 the early Hebrews & I/29a Early Philistines.

Later on the Biblical account shifts to the rivalry between the Hebrews in their new homeland and the Philistines occupying the cities along the coast. In the Bible the Philistines are the "baddies" and today we use the adjective "philistine" to denote those who take a wicked delight in destruction. This is unfair since the Philistines had their own civilisation and it was the Hebrew prophets who gleefully organised the destruction of the Philistine temples and priests. However even the Biblical account makes it clear that the Philistines were worthy opponents and this conflict should be an interesting one between two evenly matched sides.

I/27 Early Hebrew Army c1250-1000 BC: 1 x General (3/4Ax), 2 x Simeonites or Ephraimites (3Wb), 1 x Benjaminite archers or slingers (3Bw or Ps), 2 x Gadite or Issacharian skirmishing javelinmen (Ps), 5 x other tribesmen (3Ax), 1 x picked men or retained mercenaries (4Ax) or other tribesmen (3Ax or Ps).

Terrain Type: Hilly. **Aggression:** 3. **Enemies** include I/29a the Philistines or I/20b the Canaanites

The list for the early Hebrew army covers the period from the selection of Joshua as Judge until David's accession as King and is largely based on the Bible - which, unreliable as this may be as history, is often the only source available. The Simeonites and Ephraimites were described as "mighty men of valour" while the Benjaminites were archers or slingers. Gadites and Issacharians were skirmishers and scouts probably armed with javelins. The other tribes are best represented as Auxilia. Picked men are those selected by Gideon, mercenaries those hired by Saul.

I/29a Early Philistine Army 1166-1100 BC: 1 x General in 2-horse chariot (LCh) or on foot (4Bd), 1 x 2 horse 2 crew chariot (LCh), 6 x swordsmen (3Bd), 2 x javelinmen (3Ax), 2 x slingers or archers (Ps).

Terrain Type: Arable. **Aggression**: 3.   **Enemies** include I/20b Canaanites & I/27 the early Hebrews.

The Philistines were descended from the Sea People settled in Palestine by Rameses III after their defeat in Egypt. By around 1140 BC, they had gained independence from Egypt and were expanding along the coast. Their five cities - Ashdod, Ashkelon, Ekron, Gath and Gaza - were each ruled by an independent prince, but they usually acted in consort and their council (the "sarney") could designate an overall commander. They gradually adopted Canaanite chariot tactics, but continued to field effective infantry; while generals normally riding in chariots (such as Goliath of Gath) could sometimes dismount to fight on foot.

References: *Armies of the Ancient Near East* N. Stillman & N. Tallis, *Battles of the Bible* C. Herzog & M. Gichon, *Battles of the Bible* M. Dougherty (et al), *The Military History of Ancient Israel* R. Gabriel, *The Bible as History* W. Keller, *Archaeological Study Bible* W. Kallser (ed.), *Art of Warfare in Biblical Lands* Y. Yadin.

Conflict 6: The Assyrian came down like a wolf on the fold

The Assyrian mentioned in the title was probably Ashurbanipal (668-646 BC) and the Assyrian list includes the armies involved in the major wars of Ashurbanipal between 668 and 646 BC.

I/51 Later Sargonid Assyrian Army 680-609 BC: 1 x General in 4-horse chariot (HCh), 1 x 4-horse 4-crew chariots (HCh), 2 x armoured cavalry (Cv), 1 x foot guards with large conical shields (Sp), 2 x long-shield spearmen (Sp), 2 x archers (4Bw or Ps), 2 x round-shield unarmoured spearmen (4Ax), 1 x levies (7Hd or Ps).

Terrain Type: Arable. **Aggression:** 2. **Enemies** include I/34c Hebrews, I/42 Neo-Elamites, I/44a Neo-Babylonians & I/46b Kushite Egyptians.

The conical shield carried by guardsmen was increased in size and a long pavise-like shield was introduced for spearmen, suggesting that archery was now a major danger. Some infantry now wore body armour. Unarmoured spearmen continued to carry a smaller flat round shield and are classed as Auxilia. Some archer units were twinned with the long-shield spearmen, but there is no evidence for combined units. Cavalry now wore body armour and each man now fought with both spear and bow. Horses now had protective textile trappings.

I/34c Later Hebrew Army 799-586 BC: 1 x General in 4-horse 3/4-crew chariot (HCh), 1 x 4-horse 3/4-crew chariot (HCh), 1 x Gibborim (4Ax), 7 x tribesmen (3Ax), 2 x archers or slingers (Ps).

Terrain Type: Hilly. **Aggression:** 3. **Enemies** include I/51 Assyrians & I/46b Kushite Egyptians.

Ashurbinapal (the "Asenappar" of the Bible (Ezra 4:10)) intervened in the Hebrew state of Judah. After the death of Solomon, his kingdom had split into the northern kingdom of Israel and the southern kingdom of Judah. Gibborim "mighty men" were a hereditary knightly caste descended from David's elite guard armed with spear, javelin and shield and often wearing armour.

I/42 Neo-Elamite Army 800-639 BC: 1 x General in 4-horse 3-crew chariot (HCh) or as kallapani (Mtd-3Bw), 2 x kallapani (Mtd-3Bw), 1 x horse riders (LH), 7 x archers (3Bw), 1 x spearmen (3Ax) or archers (3Bw or Ps).

Terrain Type: Hilly. **Aggression:** 2. **Enemies** include I/51 Assyrians

& I/44a Neo-Babylonians

The kingdom of Elam fought against both Babylon and Assyria and our knowledge of their army comes from Assyrian and Babylonian reliefs. Their archers are always depicted as unarmoured and shieldless, but an Assyrian source refers to "men of the bow and the shield" and to "heavily-armed archers". The kallapani were fast light flat bed carts drawn by 2 or 4 horses or mules carrying up to 3 kneeling or sitting archers swiftly around the battlefield. The only depiction of an Elamite king shows him riding on a 4-horse kallapani cart together with one of his sons (both armed with bows) and a driver. It is uncertain whether they dismounted to shoot. Horse riders rode larger horses than those of the kallapani and were armed with spear as well as bow, but had no armour or shield.

I/44a Early Neo-Babylonian Army 746-605 BC: 1 x General (HCh), 1 x 4-horse 3-crew chariot (HCh), 2 x cavalry (Cv), 1 x spearmen (4Ax), 7 x Chaldean, Aramaean or militia archers (3Bw or Ps).

Terrain Type: Arable. **Aggression: 1. Enemies** include I/51 Assyrians & I/42 Neo-Elamites.

The Babylonian list covers the armies of Babylon during their revolts against Assyrian rule. Babylonian cavalry in Assyrian reliefs are apparently unarmoured and their horses without felt trappings.

I/46b Kushite Egyptian Army 727-664 BC: 1 x General in 4-horse 3-crew chariot (HCh), 1 x 4-horse 3-crew chariots (HCh), 2 x cavalry (Cv), 1 x Kushite javelinmen (3Ax), 2 x archers (Ps or 3Bw), 2 x Meshwesh Libyan settler militia (Sp), 1 x Libu javelinmen (3Ax) or archers (Ps), 1 x Egyptian spearmen (4Ax), 1 x Egyptian archers (4Bw).

Terrain Type: Littoral. **Aggression:** 3. **Enemies** include I/51 Assyrians & I/34c Hebrews.

Nubian "Kush" had been lost to Egypt, but around 730 BC, the Kushites counterattacked and in 712 BC, their king extended his rule to the whole of Egypt. Later wars with Assyria ended in defeat for the Kushites, who were driven out of Egypt by Ashurbanipal in 664 BC. Assyrian reliefs depict charioteers, archers and other infantry carrying javelins and smallish round shields. Few are armoured, possibly only officers. Nubian royal monuments show many ridden horses.

References: *Armies of the Ancient Near East* N. Stillman & N. Tallis, *Battles of the Bible* C. Herzog & M. Gichon.

Conflict 7: Cyrus the Great and Croesus of Lydia c547 BC.

Croesus was king of Lydia (in south-west Turkey) from 560 BC to 547 BC. He is renowned for his wealth and was said to have produced the first gold coins. Before attacking Cyrus, Croesus consulted the Delphic oracle to find out what the result would be. The oracle replied that if he did so "a mighty empire would fall" but carefully did not specify which empire that would be.

Cyrus the Great became king of Persia around 550 BC and started to build his empire by conquering the Medes. His ambition was seen as a threat by his neighbours, especially Croesus in nearby Lydia. Croesus made an alliance with Sparta and together they attacked the Persian empire. The first battle was inconclusive and both sides retreated. However while Croesus assumed the conflict was over until the next year, Cyrus continued in to the winter, attacked Croesus near Sardis and conquered him. There are differing accounts of what happened to Croesus after this, some say he was burnt alive on a pyre by Cyrus, others that Cyrus reprieved him and kept him as a slave to advise him in his future conquests.

I/50 Lydian Army 687-540 BC: 1 x General in 2-horse 2-crew chariot (LCh) or on horseback (3Kn), 2 x Lydian cavalry (3Kn), 2 x Phrygian or Paphlagonian light horse (LH), 4 x pre-hoplite spearmen (Sp or 4Ax), 3 x javelinmen, archers or slingers (Ps).

Terrain Type: Hilly. **Aggression:** 1. **Enemies** include I/60a, I/60b (two versions of Cyrus the Great's army).

The Lydian list covers the Lydian kingdom in Asia Minor from the overthrow of the Phrygian Maeonian dynasty in a palace coup by the native Gyges around 687 BC until the defeat of his descendant Croesus by Cyrus the Great in 540 BC and the incorporation of Lydia into the Persian empire. The Lydians also used large numbers of mercenary and provincial troops from the surrounding area.

I/60b Cyrus' Army from the Cyropaedia 546-540 BC: 1 x General (Cv), 1 x cavalry (Cv), 1 x scythed chariots (SCh), 5 x sparabara (8Bw), 1 x mobile tower (WWg), 1 x camelry (Cm), 1 x Armenians or similar (3Ax), 1 x archers (Ps).

Terrain Type: Arable. **Aggression:** 3. **Enemy:** I/50 Lydian army.

Xenophon's Cyropaedia has been described as "the first historical novel" and its troop descriptions are often regarded sceptically.

However, he had fought a Persian army, there is nothing impossible about them and I/60b provides fun games for both sides

After his conquest of Lydia, Cyrus continued on his victorious career. He attacked the Babylonians and then moved into central Asia, building up the Persian or Achaemenid empire before his death fighting the Massagetae.

I/60a Achaemenid Army 550-547 BC: 1 x General in 2-horse 2-crew chariot (LCh) or on horseback (Cv), 1 x cavalry (Cv), 1 x cavalry (Cv or LH), 1 x Immortals (8Bw), 3 x other sparabara (8Bw), 1 x Armenians or similar (3Ax), 2 x archers (3Bw or Ps), 2 x levies (7Hd).

Terrain Type: Arable. **Aggression:** 3. **Enemies** include I/43c Massagetae & I/50 Lydian Army.

The Persian lists cover the Persian armies from Cyrus the Great's defeat of the Medes until the abandonment of sparabara infantry. Sparabara were archer units fronted by men with short spear and big rectangular cane shield, so better able to survive close combat; represented by a double element (8Bw) with spearmen in front and archers behind. The elite Immortals can be distinguished by scale instead of textile corselets and possibly all bowmen also having spears. This was the army used by Cyrus the Great to build his empire.

I/43c Massagetae Army 550-150 BC: 1 x General (Cv), 1 x noble cavalry on armoured horses (Cv), 7 x horse archers (LH), 2 x archers (3Bw or Ps), 1 x subject tribesmen (3Ax or 7Hd).

Terrain Type: Steppe. **Aggression:** 2. **Enemies** include I/60a Cyrus' army.

This list covers one of the early horse-archer nations, the Massagetae. All these had large numbers of horse-archers and also sometimes used subject tribesmen in their armies. Nobles wore armour and carried lances.

References: *Armies of the Ancient Near East* N. Stillman & N. Tallis, *The Cyropaedia* Xenophon, *The Histories* Herodotos, *The Achaemenid Persian Army* D. Head, *Persian Fire* T. Holland, *Shadow of Wings* R.F. Tapsell (novel), *The Last King of Lydia* T. Leach (novel).

Conflict 8: Greeks and Persians 490-478BC

The Greek city states fought incessantly among themselves for many years, until they were rudely interrupted by the Persians. Only two of the Greek armies are included here, but the full DBA list includes many more.

I first met the Greeks of this period at school, where the Athenians, being the "inventors of democracy" were the "good guys". I became less impressed when I discovered that their definition of democracy involved the free citizens of Athens lounging around the agora (market place) and gossiping among themselves while the women and slaves stayed at home and did all the work! The Spartans were "less democratic" which seems to mean that they spent less time talking. Spartan boys and girls received a similar education and were trained to a high level of physical fitness, but there was still a rigid distinction between the citizens (Spartiates) and the other inhabitants (the perioikoi and helots). The other Greek cities of the period had the same idea that the Greeks, and especially the citizens of their own city, were vastly superior to everyone else and were especially scathing about the "Barbaroi" who spoke their own languages rather than Greek.

I/52b Spartan Hoplite Army 668-449 BC: 1 x General (Sp), 10 x citizen hoplites (Sp), 1 x perioikoi hoplites (Sp) or massed armed helots (7Hd).

Terrain Type: Arable. **Aggression**: 2. **Enemies** include I/52f Athenians & I/60c Persians.

I/52f Later Athenian Hoplite Army 540-449 BC: 1 x General (Sp), 7 x hoplites (Sp), 1 x Thessalians (Cv or LH) or hoplites (Sp), 1 x Thracians (Ps) or hoplites (Sp), 1 x archers (Ps or 3Bw), 1 x psiloi or seamen (Ps).

Terrain Type: Littoral. **Aggression**: 2. **Enemies** include I/52b Spartans & I/60c Persians.

The hoplite system depended on the combination of a large strong round wooden shield with bronze rim (the "hoplon" from which the term hoplite derives) with a long thrusting spear, bronze body-armour and usually a "Corinthian" helmet that badly restricted both sight and hearing. Most states could also field a limited number of "psiloi" (unarmoured men who skirmished with javelins, bows or slings), and mountain states had access to larger numbers of tough skirmishing hillmen with javelins and often later a small shield "pelta".

The Greek cities were united by the need to resist the Persian invasion resulting in the heroic story of Thermopylae (commemorated in books, poems and films ever since) and the battles of Salamis and Marathon. In these stories, the Persians were there merely to provide an enemy who was finally defeated.

I/60c Achaemenid Persian Army 539-420 BC: 1 x General in 2-horse chariot (LCh) or on horseback (Cv), 1 x cavalry (Cv), 1 x cavalry (Cv or LH), 1 x Immortals (8Bw or 4Bw), 3 x other archers (8Bw or 3/4Bw), 1 x Armenians or similar (3Ax), 1 x Greek hoplites (Sp), 3 x subject levies (7Hd or Ps).

Terrain Type: Arable. **Aggression:** 3. **Enemies** include I/52b Spartans & I/52f Athenians.

The Persian list covers the Persian armies from Cyrus the Great's defeat of the Medes until the abandonment of sparabara infantry and include this period. Sparabara were archer units fronted by men with short spear and big rectangular cane shield, represented by a double element (8Bw) with spearmen in front and archers behind. The elite Immortals can be distinguished by scale instead of textile corslets and possibly all bowmen also having spears. From 465 BC, sparabara started to be replaced by ordinary archers with axe and crescent-shaped shield.

More recently, some of the histories and novels have taken the Persian side. Our list of references helps you to follow up on this.

References: *Armies of the Greek and Persian Wars* R.Nelson, *The Western Way of War* V.D Hanson, *The Wars of the Ancient Greeks* V.D Hanson, *Persian Fire* T. Holland, *The Defence of Greece* J.F Lazenby, *The Rise of the Greeks* M. Grant, *Greece and Rome at War* P. Connolly, *The Histories* Herodotos, *Slingshot* 96, 97, 98, 100, 101, 102, *The Achaemenid Persian Army* D. Head, *The Cyropaedia* Xenophon, *The Gates of Fire* S.Pressfield, *Killer of Men & Marathon* C. Cameron (novels)., *Shadow of Wings* R.F. Tapsell (novel), online references in Wikipedia and elsewhere.

Conflict 9: Ancient India.

The proto-Indian or Harappan civilisation of the Indus valley of western India was known to the Mesopotamians as "the land of Melukhkha", but their own name for themselves is not known. They provided sea-borne forces for the Great Revolt against Akkad and for the enemies of the Third Dynasty of Ur. The Indus civilisation collapsed around 1900 BC and was replaced by the less urbanised pre-Vedic culture which lasted until about 1500 BC. In the published accounts of excavations at Mohenjo-Daro, Michael Jansen, one of the many excavators of their cities, says that they had no armies. However, numerous weapon finds include heavy spear heads, axes, dirks, arrowheads and baked clay slingshot, the latter especially associated with town defences. A rectangular shield is possibly represented on one seal.

I/10 Melukhkhan or pre-Vedic Indian Army 2700-1500 BC: 1 x General (3Pk or Sp), 3 x spearmen (3Pk or Sp), 2 x archers (4Bw), 2 x archers (4Bw) or Kulli highlanders (3Ax), 4 x slingers (Ps).

Terrain Type: Littoral. **Aggression**: 0. **Enemies** include I/23a Early Vedic Indians.

Around 1500 BC, the Aryan invasion of northern India included the Indus valley and included conflict with the existing inhabitants. Their army is described in the early Vedic list.

I/23a Early Vedic Indian Army 1500-900 BC: 1 x General (LCh), 4 x heroic charioteers (LCh), 5 x archers (3Bw), 2 x followers (7Hd).

Terrain Type: Tropical. **Aggression**: 2. **Enemies** include I/10 pre-Vedic Indians and I/23a (each other).

The Vedic lists cover Indian armies from the Aryan invasion of India to the north until the Persian conquest of the north-west and the establishment of the first Buddhist states Most chariots had two unarmoured horses and were crewed by a driver and an armoured noble archer. In the later period, the general might have a heavy chariot with a parasol, 4 horses and up to 4 crew. Other foot were mostly archers who clumped at the rear and tried to avoid hand-to-hand combat.

The main sources are the Vedas and the Mahabharata which include descriptions of many battles, mostly between each other. Some of the accounts probably describe their conquest of the Indus valley as well as their resistance to the Persian invasion and the establishment of the

Buddhist states.

I/23b Later Vedic Indian Army 899-501 BC: 1 x General (LCh or HCh), 1 x elephant (El) or charioteer (LCh), 4 x heroic charioteers (LCh), 5 x archers (3Bw), 1 x followers (7Hd).

Terrain Type: Tropical. **Aggression:** 2. **Enemies** include I/60a Achaemenids and I/23b (each other).

This is the army who fought against Darius the Great when he invaded India in 512-515 BC. Historically they were unsuccessful and Darius gained control of the Indus Valley before returning to Persia.

I/60c Achaemenid Army 539-420 BC: 1 x General in 2-horse chariot (LCh) or on horseback (Cv), 1 x cavalry (Cv), 1 x cavalry (Cv or LH), 1 x Immortals (8Bw or 4Bw), 3 x other archers (8Bw or 3/4Bw), 1 x Armenians or similar (3Ax), 1 x Greek hoplites (Sp), 3 x subject levies (7Hd or Ps).

Terrain Type: Arable. **Aggression:** 3. **Enemies** include I/23b Vedic Indians.

This Achaemenid list covers Persian armies until the abandonment of sparabara infantry. Sparabara were archer units (8Bw) fronted by men with short spear and big rectangular cane shield, represented by a double element rank with spearmen in front and archers behind. The elite Immortals can be distinguished by scale instead of textile corslets and possibly by all bowmen also having spears.

References: *Armies of the Ancient Near East* N. Stillman & N. Tallis, *Armies of the Macedonian and Punic Wars* D. Head, *The Mahabharata* R.K. Narayan, *Ancient Indian Warfare* S.D. Singh, *The Achaemenid Persian Army* D. Head, *Warfare in the Ancient Near East* W.Hamblin. Translations of the Vedas and the Mahabharata including information online and a recent TV series.

Conflict 10: Alexander the Great 336 BC – 323 BC.

Inheriting the throne of Macedon after his father's death, Alexander spent some time getting control of his own kingdom and the surrounding Greek cities. He then moved east to confront Darius and the Persian empire.

II/12 Alexandrian Macedonian Army 359-319 BC: 1 x General and companions (3Kn), 1 x Thessalians (Cv), 1 x light horse (LH), 1 x hypaspists (4Ax), 6 x phalangites (4Pk), 1 x psiloi (Ps), 1 x Greek hoplites (Sp) or Thracians (3/4Ax) or bolt-shooters (Art).

Terrain Type: Arable. **Aggression:** 4. **Enemies** include II/7 Darius' army.

The list covers the armies used in the battles against the Persians. The Macedonian "pezetairos" phalangites were equipped with an 18 foot sarissa held in both hands, a round shield smaller than that of hoplites, helmet and greaves and are classed as pike. The hypaspists had hoplite shield, helmet, greaves and light body armour and carried the longche (a dual-purpose throwing and thrusting spear). The psiloi are Agrianian javelinmen, Macedonian or Cretan archers and Rhodian slingers.

II/7 Darius' Army (Later Achaemenid Persian 430-329 BC): 1 x General in 2-horse 2-crew chariot (LCh) or on horseback (Cv or 3Kn), 2 x Persian, Median or Bactrian cavalry (Cv), 2 x light horse (LH), 2 x Bactrian or Saka noble armoured horse cavalry (3Kn) or mercenary hoplites (Sp) or Kardakes (4Ax), 1 x scythed chariot (SCh) or mercenary hoplites (Sp), 1 x archers or slingers (Ps), 2 x kardakes (4Ax) or takabara (3Ax) or mercenary hoplites (Sp) or Saka horse archers (LH), 1 x subject conscript masses (7Hd or Ps).

Terrain Type: Arable. **Aggression:** 1. **Enemies** include II/12 Alexander's army

Darius' army is depicted on the Alexander mosaic in Pompeii (also on the DBMM cover). The soldiers were dressed bright colours and all ranks wore a dark-yellow headdress. Most cavalry were armed with javelins and none had shields. Greek mercenary hoplites were extensively used. Kardakes were the new standard "takabara" infantry type, each armed with 2 javelins, a bow and a wicker pelta or a hoplite shield. These were backed by good quality skirmishers with bows or slings and masses of subject conscripts. Scythed chariots were a standard part of the army. After his victory over Darius, Alexander went on to establish an empire with a capital at Babylon and also reorganised his army to include troops from the conquered territories. The next list covers the army of Alexander the Great fighting in India.

II/15. Alexandrian Imperial Army 328-321 BC: 1 x General (3Kn), 1 x companions (3Kn), 1 x Asiatic light horse (LH), 6 x argyraspids and phalagites (4Pk), 1 x bolt-shooters (Art) or elephants (El), 1 x Thracians, Illyrians or Agrianians (3/4Ax or Ps), 1 x archers or slingers (Ps).

Terrain Type: Arable. **Aggression**: 4. **Enemies** include II/3a Porus' army.

The Companions now included the prodromoi together with the pick of the Persians. Scouting cavalry were Asiatic light horse while the hypaspists were now pike-armed and had become the "argyraspids" (silver shields).

II/3a Porus' Army 328 BC-321 BC: 1 x General (Porus) (El), 2 x elephants (El), 2 x 2-horse 2-crew (LCh) or 4-horse 3 or 6-crew chariots (HCh), 2 x cavalry (Cv), 3 x archers (3Lb), 1 x javelinmen (4Ax), 1 x levies (7Hd) or wild tribes archers (Ps).

Terrain Type: Tropical. **Aggression**: 0. **Enemies** include II/15 Alexander's army

This Indian list describes the army used by Porus against Alexander. Elephant crew sat astride on a padded caparison and consisted of a driver and a single noble archer. The large 4-horse 6-crew chariots may have been part of Poros' army and manned by 2 javelin-armed drivers, 2 archers and 2 shield-bearers while other rulers used 4-horse chariots with a crew of a driver & two archers. The cavalry were javelin-armed and unarmoured. The Indian bow was long and shot heavy arrows. Archers and javelinmen also carried a heavy two-handed sword. Good infantry were supplemented with a massed horde of levies or "Wild tribes" of hillmen or jungle-dwellers who could provide skirmishers.

References: *Armies of the Macedonian and Punic Wars* D. Head, *Alexander the Great's Campaigns* P. Barker, *Alexander the Great* R. Lane Fox, *Alexander at the World's End* T. Holt (novel). *The Achaemenid Persian Army* D. Head. *An Elephant for Aristotle* L. Sprague de Camp (novel), *A Choice of Destinies* M. Scott (novel). *Ancient Indian Warfare* S.D Singh, *History of Alexander* and *Indica* Arrian (and other histories of Alexander), *The Arthashastra* Kautilya, *Creation* G.Vidal (novel).

Conflict 11: Early China (the terracotta army).

This list covers all the armies of the Warring States period up to the victory of Ch'in over its rivals in 221 BC.

Generals and nobility rode 4-horse heavy chariots, each crewed by a driver, archer and halberdier. Massed conscript infantry were stiffened by armoured elite troops, as shown by the Ch'in terracotta army. Early infantry were depicted carrying very long ji-halberds or spears and no shields while archers shot from behind them. Peasants were said to need little training to use these pole-arms, using horizontal reaping strokes against chariots and vertical hoeing strokes against foot (they are classed as Pk).

It also includes the Ch'in empire from 220 BC until its collapse in 207 BC; and then the wars of succession until the establishment of the Han dynasty in 202 BC.

After the mid-4th century, the dominant infantry weapon was the crossbow. The spears and dagger-axes used by close-fighting infantry were now much shorter and often used with shields, so they are classed as Auxilia or Blades, except in Ch'in armies, where a system of promotion based on enemy heads taken produced fanaticism that justifies Warband.

II/4a Ch'in Chinese Army 355 BC-221 BC: 1x General in 4-horse 3-crew chariot (HCh), 1 x chariots (HCh), 1 x cavalry (Cv), 4 x infantry (4Wb), 3 x crossbowmen (3/4Cb), 1 x archers (Ps) or horse archers (LH), 1 x archers (Ps).

Terrain Type: Arable. **Aggression:** 3. **Enemies** include II/4b Yueh, II/4c Chao and II/4e other Chinese armies.

II/4b Yueh Chinese Army 480 BC-333 BC: 1 x General in 4-horse 3-crew chariot (HCh), 4 x ji-halberdiers (3Pk), 2 x crossbowmen (4Cb) or archers (Ps), 2 x ji-halberdiers (3Pk) or southern tribesmen (3Wb), 3 x archers (Ps).

Terrain Type: Arable. **Aggression:** 1. **Enemies** include II/4a Ch'in and II/4e other Chinese armies.

II/4c Chao Chinese Army 307 BC-202 BC: 1 x General in 4-horse 3-crew chariot (HCh) or on horseback (Cv), 1 x 4-horse 3-crew chariots (HCh) or horse archers (LH), 2 x horse archers (LH), 3 x crossbowmen (4Cb), 4 x short dagger-axe (4Bd) or spearmen (4Ax), 1 x archers (Ps).

Terrain Type: Arable. **Aggression:** 1. **Enemies** include II/4a Ch'in and II/4e other Chinese armies.

II/4e Other Chinese Armies 355 BC-202 BC: 1 x General in 4-horse 3-crew chariot (HCh) or on horseback (Cv), 1 x chariot 4-horse 3-crew (HCh) or archers (Ps), 1 x cavalry (Cv) or horse archers (LH) or archers (Ps), 2 x crossbowmen (4Cb), 2 x close-fighters (4Ax or 4Bd), 1 x swordsmen or clubmen (3Bd) or archers (Ps), 4 x crossbowmen (3/4Cb) or close-fighters (4Ax or 4Bd) or hasty levies (7Hd) or peasant rebels (5Hd).

Terrain Type: Arable. Aggression: 1. **Enemies** include II/4a Ch'in, II/4b Yueh, II/4c Chao and II/4e each other.

References: *Ancient Chinese Armies* C. Peers, *The Art of War* Sun Tzu, *The Perilous Frontier* T.J Barfield.

Conflict 12: Pyrrhos of Epiros 319 BC – 272 BC.

Born in the turmoil following the death of Alexander the Great, Pyrrhus spent much of his early life in exile and when he did succeed to the kingdom of Epirus he then competed with Demetrius for control of Macedonia. During his time in Macedonia, he had a traditional Epirot army as shown here:

II/27a Pyrrhic Army 300-281BC: 1 x General (Pyrrhos) (3Kn), 1 x cavalry (Cv), 6 x phalangites (4Pk), 2 x Aitoilan or similar javelinmen (Ps), 2 x archers or slingers (Ps).

Terrain Type: Arable. **Aggression**: 4. **Enemies** include II/16b Demetrios' army.

His main opponent was Demetrios Poliorketes "the Besieger" whose army was very similar to that of Pyrrhos. His heavy cavalry and light horse were of assorted Asiatic types. His pike phalanx was officered by Macedonians, but those in its ranks were mostly new recruits. Having few genuine Macedonians, they had to be supplemented with retrained Greek hoplites and peltasts and later by Asiatic "pantodapoi". Light troops were all barbarians or Asiatics.

II/16b Demetrios' Army 315-285 BC: 1 x General (Demetrios) (3Kn), 1 x light horse (LH), 6 x phalangites (4Pk), 1 x peltasts (3/4Ax), 2 x Greek ally hoplites (Sp) or [1 x cavalry (Cv) + 1 x elephants (El)], 1 x archers, slingers or javelinmen (Ps) or bolt-shooters or stone-throwers (Art).

Terrain Type: Littoral.   **Aggression**: 3. **Enemies** include II/27a Pyrrhos of Epirus.

Around 280 BC, a complicated assortment of treaties resulted in Pyrrhus being employed to bring an army and assist the Italiot Greek cities against the Romans. Pyrrhos not only reorganised the Epeirot infantry into Macedonian-style phalangites, but was probably responsible for the spread of shields among the Hellenistic cavalry, which could not be used with the xyston. However, Plutarch described him as personally still using the xyston in his last battles. Pyrrhus won a series of battles against the Romans and the high losses in these battles are the origin of the term "Pyrrhic Victory"

II/27b Pyrrhic Army 280-272BC: 1 x General (Pyrrhos)(3Kn or Cv), 1 x Greek or Oscan cavalry (Cv), 1 x Tarentines (LH), 1 x elephants (El), 4 x phalangites (4Pk), 2 x Italiot hoplites (Sp) or Tarentine phalangites (4Pk), 1 x Oscan foot (3/4Ax) or from 275 BC Galatians (4Wb), 1 x archers or slingers (Ps).

Terrain Type: Arable. **Aggression:** 4. **Enemies** include I/61b Carthagianian & II/10 Camillan Roman

The Roman list describes the Roman armies who opposed Pyrrhos. Roman armies were still citizen levies, but were increasingly kept in the field for long periods and paid while in service. Cavalry fought with spears and small round shields. Each legion usually had shieldless leves skirmishing in front with javelins, followed by hastati with pila, sword and scutum, then by principes with long spear, sword & scutum, and finally by a reserve of veteran triarii armed like the principes. Unassimilated Italian allies should be depicted as Oscans.

II/10 Camillan Roman Army 400-275 BC: 1 x General (Cv), 1 x cavalry (Cv), 2 x leves (Ps), 2 x hastati (4Bd), 2 x principes (Sp), 2 x triarii (Sp), 2 x unassimilated Italian allies (3Ax or 4Ax).

Terrain Type: Arable. **Aggression:** 3. **Enemies** include II/27b Pyrrhos.

After these campaigns, Pyrrhos then moved to Sicily and fought the Carthaginians. The city of Carthage had started as a colony planted on the North African coast by a Phoenician rebel Queen, Dido. It grew into a powerful trading state, which would later become Rome's most dangerous rival. Eventually returning home to Macedonia, Pyrrhos was killed by a woman throwing a tile from a roof top.

I/61b Early Carthaginian Army 340-275 BC: 1 x General on foot (Sp) or on horseback (Cv) or in 4-horse 3-man chariot (HCh), 1 x 4-horse 3-man chariots (HCh), 1 x cavalry (Cv), 1 x Numidians (LH) or Spanish (4Ax), 2 x citizen and/or African spearmen (Sp), 2 x African spearmen (Sp), 1 x mercenary hoplites (Sp) or Spanish (4Ax), 1 x Gauls (4Wb) or Sicels (3Ax), 2 x skirmishing javelinmen, slingers or archers (Ps).

Terrain Type: Littoral. **Aggression:** 3. **Enemies** include II/27b Pyrrhic army.

References and further reading: *Armies of the Macedonian and Punic Wars* D. Head, *The Punic Wars* A. Goldsworthy. *The Making of the Roman Army* L. Keppie, *The Wars of Alexander's Successors Vols 1 & 2* B. Bennett & M. Roberts, *Pyrrhus of Epirus* J. Champion, *Elephants and Castles* A. Duggan (novel), *The Bronze God of Rhodes* L. Sprague de Camp (novel), *Funeral Games* M. Renault (novel).

Conflict 13: The Punic Wars.

The Punic Wars were a struggle between Rome and Carthage, both of whom wished to control the Mediterranean and its trade. Initially Carthage had the advantage with its armies raised from north Africa and Spain but Rome gradually gained the upper hand. My first encounter with this period was the musical "Jupiter's Darling", shown as a film in the 1950s, which was a colourful and wildly inaccurate account of Hannibal's march on Rome. Later I came to the more mundane but more accurate historical accounts, mentioned in the references or to be found online.

II/32a Later Carthaginian Army 275-202 BC: 1 x General (Cv), 1 x cavalry (Cv) or elephants (El), 1 x elephants (El) or light horse (LH), 1 x Numidians (LH), 3 x Libyan or Poeni spearmen (Sp), 1 x Spanish scutati or Ligurians (4Ax), 2 x Gauls (4Wb/4Ax) or Spanish scutati (4Ax), 1 x African or Spanish caetrati javelinmen (Ps), 1 x slingers (Ps).

Terrain Type: Littoral. **Aggression:** 4. **Enemies** include II/33 Polybian Roman

II/32b Later Carthaginian Army 201-146 BC: 1 x General on horseback (Cv) or on foot (Sp), 1 x cavalry (Cv), 1 x Numidians (LH) or Poeni spearmen (Sp), 6 x Poeni spearmen (Sp), 3 x javelinmen (Ps).

Terrain Type: Littoral. **Aggression:** 1. **Enemy:** II/33 Polybian Roman

The later Carthaginian army was largely regular Libyan spearmen and Spanish and Gallic mercenaries. All horsemen now used shield and javelins. Cavalry became a mix of Poeni (Carthaginian citizens), Spanish, Gauls and Italians. The number of Numidian Light Horse shrank when their ruler changed sides in 205 BC. Spanish foot were mostly scutati with long shields, the rest caetrati with small round shields. At the Trebia in 218 BC, Hannibal's Gallic foot fought under tribal leaders and are classed as Wb. At Cannae in 216 BC, they were organised in small units and mixed with Spanish and so can alternatively be 4Ax. The elephants Hannibal took to Italy over the Alps quickly died and replacements were infrequent. At Zama in 202 BC, larger numbers of inadequately-trained elephants were used as an expendable front line.

II/33   Polybian Roman Army 275-105 BC: 1 x General (Cv), 1 x equites (Cv), 4 x hastati/principes (4Bd), 2 x hastati/principes (4Bd) or allies (3/4Ax), 2 x triarii (Sp), 2 x velites (Ps).

Terrain Type: Arable. **Aggression**: 3.   **Enemies** include II/32a and II/32b Carthaginian

Roman armies were raised annually by the two consuls but those serving overseas often served for longer periods. A consular army was normally 2 legions, supported by the same number of allied alae (or wings).

Each legion should be deployed with the velites skirmishing in front with javelins, then the hastati and principes, each of whom had a pilum (a heavy throwing spear capable of penetrating armour or immobilising an enemy's shield), a gladius (a short Spanish sword ideal for thrusting past your own shield), a scutum (a large stout oval shield), bronze helmet and either a mail shirt or small rectangular breastplate.

At the rear were a reserve of veteran triarii still armed with long spear instead of pilum.

References: *Armies of the Macedonian and Punic Wars* D. Head, *The Punic Wars* A. Goldsworthy, *The First Punic War* J.F Lazenby, *Hannibal's War* J.F. Lazenby, *Hannibal's Campaigns* T. Bath, *The Second Punic War A Reappraisal* T. Cornell, B. Rankov & P. Sabin. *The Making of the Roman Army* L. Keppie, *The Complete Roman Army* A. Goldsworthy, *Scipio Africanus: Soldier and Politician* H.H. Scullard.

Conflict 14: Rome moves East.

Having settled their account with Carthage, Rome now turned her attention to the east, where the Greeks and Macedonians were continuing in their normal disorganised fashion and just asking (in Roman eyes) to be taken over and organised into a tidy law-abiding Roman province.

II/33 Polybian Roman Army 275-105 BC: 1 x General (Cv), 1 x equites (Cv), 4 x hastati/principes (4Bd), 2 x hastati/principes (4Bd) or allies (3/4Ax), 2 x triarii (Sp), 2 x velites (Ps).

Terrain Type: Arable. **Aggression:** 3. **Enemies** include II/19c Seleucids and II/35 Macedonians.

The same armies which had dealt with the Carthaginians, now turned their attention to Macedonia. In the Roman armies each legion was deployed with the velites skirmishing in front with javelins, then the hastati and principes, each of whom had a pilum, a gladius, a scutum, a bronze helmet and either a mail shirt or small rectangular breastplate. At the rear were a reserve of veteran triarii still armed with long spear instead of pilum.

II/35 Later Macedonian Army 260-148 BC: 1 x General (Cv), 1 x Greek or Galatian cavalry (Cv) 1 x Greek or Illyrian javelin-armed light horse (LH), 2 x brazen shields (4Pk), 4 x white shields (4Pk), 2 x thorakitai or thureophoroi (4Ax) or Akarnanian javelinmen (Ps), 1 x Cretan archers (Ps) or Thracians (4Ax) or Galatians (4Wb).

Terrain Type: Arable. **Aggression:** 1. **Enemies** include II/19c Seleucid and II/33 Romans.

Macedon was in a difficult position, with Rome on one side, the Seleucid empire on the other and no sign of another Alexander to come to their aid. The Macedonian list covers the period until the incorporation of Macedonia as a Roman province. Chalkaspides "brazen/bronze shields" included both the Agema and another unit of guard pikemen called "Peltasts". Non-guard phalangites were called leukaspides "White Shields". Cavalry were now armed with javelins and shield instead of xyston. The auxilia consisted of Macedonian thureophoroi and thorakitai and Thracian mercenaries.

Once Rome had settled Macedon, she then found herself with the Seleucids on her new border and they were trouble. The war with the Seleucid empire continued for many years until finally overcome by

Pompey, Julius Caesar's great rival.

II/19c Seleucid Army 204-167 BC: 1 x General (3/4Kn), 1 x cataphracts (4Kn), 4 x phalangites (4Pk), 1 x elephants (El), 1 x scythed chariot (SCh), 1 x thureophoroi (4Ax) or Thracians (3Ax), 1 x thureophoroi (4Ax) or Galatians (4Wb), 2 x Asiatic archers and slingers (Ps).

Terrain Type: Arable. **Aggression**: 2. **Enemies** include II/33 Romans and II/35 Macedonians

The complete Seleucid lists cover the kingdom from its foundation by Alexander's general Seleukos until its abolition by Pompey. This list II/19c refers to the period of this conflict and includes the major battles at Thermopylae and Magnesia. Most of the Xystophoroi were converted into cataphracts after the war with the Parthians.

References: *Armies of the Macedonian and Punic Wars* D. Head. *The Making of the Roman Army* L. Keppie, *The Complete Roman Army* A. Goldsworthy, References: *Armies of the Macedonian and Punic Wars* D. Head, *The Wars of Alexander's Successors Vols 1&2* B. Bennett & M. Roberts, *The Seleucid Army: Organisation & Tactics in the Great Campaigns* B. Bar-Kochva, *The Seleucid Army* N. Sekunda, *Funeral Games* M. Renault (novel).

Conflict 15: Spartacus revolts against Rome

Slavery was commonplace in the ancient world and as Rome's conquests continued, the number of slaves increased until they greatly outnumbered the free population. Penalties for revolt were immediate and extreme and on the whole the slaves accepted their fate. Although single individuals were unable to do anything against the might of Rome, occasionally the slaves combined and caused a more serious problem.

There were three major slave revolts against the Romans, two in Sicily and the third (led by Spartacus) in Italy, largely around Mount Vesuvius. The two Sicilian revolts were marked by extreme rivalry and treachery between slave commanders, but Spartacus seems to have avoided this problem.

II/45c Spartacus' Army in southern Italy 74-71 BC: 1 x General on horseback (Cv) or on foot (4Bd), 1 x ex-gladiators or veteran war prisoners with Roman equipment (4Bd), 1 x German or Gaul ex-slaves fighting in native style (3/4Wb), 3 x other ex-slaves with Roman equipment (4Bd), 5 x other ex-slaves (5Hd), 2 x herdsmen and shepherds (Ps).

Terrain Type: Hilly. **Aggression:** 0. **Enemy:** II/49 Marian Romans

In Spartacus' army, it is unlikely that large numbers were gladiators who had retained gladiatorial weapons. The Gauls and Germans formed distinct units and probably fought in their own native style, but not costume. The majority of ex-slaves are classed as horde (5Hd) to reflect the combination of desperation (surrender meant death) and shortage of equipment. Plutarch mentions the use of herdsmen and shepherds as skirmishers, probably with slings.

Not surprisingly, the Roman populace was terrified by the revolt of the slaves and hastily summoned the Roman army to protect them and deal with the slaves.

II/49 Marian Roman Army 105-25 BC: 1 x General (Cv or 4Bd), 1 x Gallic, Spanish, Macedonian, Greek or similar auxiliary cavalry (Cv) or javelin-throwing Numidian, German, Illyrian or similar light horse (LH), 5 x legionaries (4Bd), 2 x legionaries (4Bd) or Spanish, Illyrian or similar auxiliary foot (4Ax) or Syrian horse archers (LH), 1 x German, Numidian, Spanish or similar javelinmen (Ps or 3Ax), 1 x archers or slingers (Ps), 1 x Numidian elephant (El) or wild Gauls (4Wb), cavalry (Cv) or requisitioned city bolt-shooters (Art).

Terrain Type: Arable. **Aggression:** 3. **Enemies** include II/45c Spartacus' slave revolt.

The Roman list covers the Roman armies from the reforms of Marius until those of Augustus and includes the army used to suppress Spartacus' revolt. Legionaries were now long-service regulars recruited from the poor and a farm was now the reward for service instead of the qualification to join the legions. All were armed with pilum and gladius (short mainly thrusting sword) and protected by bronze helmet, iron mail shirt and big oval scutum. Auxiliaries were equipped and fought in their own native styles. Cavalry were most often Spanish, Gallic or German, Javelin-armed light horse might be Spanish, Numidian, Thracian or Illyrian, horse archer could be Thracian or provided by Asian client rulers, skirmishing javelinmen could be Spanish caetrati, German, Numidian or Greek auxilia could be Spanish scutati, Gauls, Illyrians, Thracians or Ligurians, slingers either Greek or Balearic, archers often Cretan.

This was obviously a tragedy since there was no real possibility of Spartacus winning in the long term and creating a rebel state alongside Rome (some islands in the Mediterranean remained a haunt of pirates and a problem for the Roman empire for many years, so possibly they could have emigrated to one of these and kept their independence but there was no possibility on the mainland). This revolt has been neglected in the literature and there are few novels with Spartacus as hero. However there has been at least one film and a recent television series in which he was portrayed as a hero. The references below give background reading for the period.

References: *Rubicon* T. Holland, Slingshots 126, 127 & 128, *Armies and Enemies of Imperial Rome* P. Barker, *Winter Quarters* A. Duggan (novel), *Three's Company* A. Duggan (novel), *Spartacus* H. Fast (novel)

Conflict 16: Romans against the Germans.

This conflict (see Chapters Two and Four), arose when the Romans sought to extend their control across the Rhine into Germany. The Germans resisted fiercely and destroyed four Roman armies before being crushed by Marius in 101 BC. Their most famous victory was at the Teutoburger Wald in 9 AD when three Roman legions were ambushed and destroyed marching through the forest.

II/49 Marian Roman Army 105-25 BC: 1 x General (Cv or 4Bd), 1 x Gallic, Spanish, Macedonian, Greek or similar auxiliary cavalry (Cv) or javelin-throwing Numidian, German, Illyrian or similar light horse (LH), 5 x legionaries (4Bd), 2 x legionaries (4Bd) or Spanish, Illyrian or similar auxiliary foot (4Ax) or Syrian horse archers (LH), 1 x German, Numidian, Spanish or similar javelinmen (Ps or 3Ax), 1 x archers or slingers (Ps), 1 x Numidian elephant (El) or wild Gauls (4Wb), cavalry (Cv) or requisitioned city bolt-shooters (Art).

Terrain Type: Arable. **Aggression:** 3. **Enemies** include II/47 various early German armies & II/49 Roman Civil War.

The Marian list covers the Roman armies from the reforms of Marius until those of Augustus. Legionaries were now long-service regulars armed with pilum and gladius and protected by bronze helmet, iron mail shirt and big oval scutum. Auxiliaries were equipped and fought in their own native styles. Cavalry were most often Spanish, Gallic or German, Javelin-armed light horse might be Spanish, Numidian or Illyrian, horse archers could be Thracian or from Asian client rulers, skirmishing javelinmen could be Spanish caetrati, German, Numidian or Greek, auxilia could be Spanish scutati, Gauls, Illyrians, Thracians or Ligurians, slingers either Greek or Balearic, archers Cretan.

II/56 Early Imperial Roman Army 25 BC - 197 AD: 1 x General on horseback (Cv) or on foot (4Bd), 1 x equites (Cv), 4 x legionaries (4Bd), 3 x auxiliary pedites (4Ax), 1 x equites (Cv) or pedites (4Ax) or archers (4Bw or Ps), 1 x Numidians or Moors (LH) or symmachiarii (3Wb) or slingers (Ps) or gladiators (3Bd), 1 x lancers (3Kn) or horse archers (LH) or bolt-shooters (Art) or dromedarii (LCm).

Terrain Type: Arable. **Aggression:** 3. **Enemies** II/47 various early German armies & II/56 Roman Civil War.

The later army dates from Augustus' reorganisation. This is the period of the legionary equipped with pilum, short gladius sword, semi-cylindrical rectangular shield, iron helmet and lorica segmentata that is the popular image of the Roman legionary. Auxiliary equites (cavalry) and pedites (infantry) were armed with short spear, javelins and long swords, had more convenient oval shields bearing regimental patterns, wore mail corselets and metal helmets.

II/47a Armies of the Cimbri or Teutones 113-102 BC: 1 x General (Cv), 1 x cavalry (Cv), 9 x warriors (4Wb), 1 x skirmishers (Ps).

Terrain Type: Forest. **Aggression: 4. Enemies** include II/49 Romans.

II/47d Batavian or Cherusci Army 115 BC – 250 AD: 1 x General (Cv), 2 x heroes with long spears (4Wb) or warriors (3Wb), 7 x warriors (3Wb), 2 x skirmishers with javelins (Ps).

Terrain Type: Littoral. **Aggression:** 2. **Enemies:** II/47g other Germans, II/49 & II/56 Romans

II/47g Other Early German armies 115 BC – 250 AD: 1 x general on horseback (Cv) or on foot (4Wb), 1 x cavalry (Cv), 8 warriors (4Wb), 1 x cavalry (Cv) or skirmisher (Ps), 1 x skirmisher (Ps).

Terrain type: Forest. **Aggression:** 2. **Enemies** include II/47a, II/47d & II/47g other Germans and II/49 & II/56 Romans.

These lists cover the German tribes from the first Roman encounter with the Cimbri and Teutones. The German tribes were more varied than previously thought, and we must differentiate between 3Wb such Cherusci and Batavi who specialised in ambushes from woods or marsh and 4Wb known as stubborn hand-to-hand fighters in close formation with a light spear called a "framea" and shield and wore trousers and usually a shirt. Red and blue dyes are archaeologically attested for the better-off warriors, but commoners may have mostly worn un-dyed natural wool. Skirmishers were otherwise usually youngsters with javelins, but a minority could be older men with bows.

References: *Armies and Enemies of Imperial Rome* P. Barker, *Ancient Germanic Warriors* M.P. Speidel, *Germania* Tacitus, *Rubicon* T. Holland, *The Roman Army at War 100BC-200AD* A. Goldsworthy, *The Long Year AD 69* K. Wellesley, *The Roman Legions Recreated in Colour* D. Peterson, *Votan* J. James (novel), *Winter Quarters* A. Duggan (novel), *Three's Company* A. Duggan (novel), *Imperial Governor* G. Shipway (novel), *The Provincial Governor* J. Scott (novel), *Year of the Four Ceasars* H.Nield (novel), *Nobody Loves a Centurian* J.M.Roberts (novel) & *The Iron Hand of Mars* L.Davis (novel).

Conflict 17: Romans in the East

This is an interesting triangle with the Palmyrans first aiding the Romas against the Sassanids and later seeking independence. The conflict started in 259 AD when the Roman emperor Valerian was defeated by Shapur, the Sassanid king.

II/64b Eastern Roman Army 193-324 AD: 1 x General (Cv), 1 x cavalry (Cv), 1 x eastern horse archers (LH), 4 x legionaries (4Bd), 3 x auxiliaries (4Ax), 1 x auxiliaries (4Ax) or archers (4Bw or Ps), 1 x clibanarii (4Kn) or legionaries (4Bd) or lanciarii (3Bd) or bolt-shooters (Art).

Terrain Type: Arable. **Aggression:** 2. **Enemies** include II/69b Sassanid Persian and II/74b Zenobia of Palmyra.

Legionary armour was now a knee-length heavy coat of mail and helmets with large cheek pieces. The long spatha had replaced the gladius and shields were now a large heavy near round oval. The excavation at Dura Europus included shields with the inside a dull red and painted patterns on the outside. The heavy legionary equipment led to intermediate type of infantry armed with the light lancea (the "lancearius"). A tombstone shows a lanciarius as unarmoured and carrying a small shield and 5 light throwing spears. The javelin-armed light horse included the Equites Illyriciani, Dalmatae, Moors and scutarii. Heavier cavalry continued much as before and now included completely armoured lancers on fully scale-armoured horses called clibanarii. Tunics were long-sleeved, white or red and trousers are usually depicted as dark brown. Cloaks were yellow-brown "russus".

II/69b Sassanid Persian Army 225-493 AD: : 1 x General (Cv), 1 x cataphracts (4Kn), 4 x asavaran (Cv), 1 x elephants (El) or asavaran (Cv), 1 x asavaran (Cv) or nomad or vassal horse archers (LH), 1 x asavaran (Cv) or archers and slingers (Ps), 1 x nomad or vassal horse archers (LH) or Arabs (LH) or Dailami (4Ax) or other hillmen (3Ax), 2 x levies (7Hd).

Terrain Type: Arable. **Aggression:** 3. **Enemies** include II/64b Eastern Roman and II/74a Odenathus of Palmyra.

The Sassanid lists cover the Sassanid dynasty of Persia. A limited number of Parthian style cataphracts (4Kn) provided a striking force of lancers in full metal armour and masked helmets riding metal-armoured horses. The strength of the army was the asavaran who wore mail shirts, rode horses in full leather or felt protection (or metal half-armour) and were armed with bow and heavy sword. Peasant levy spearmen with rectangular cane-reinforced rawhide shields formed a rear line in battle. Vassal nations provided horse archers and Dailami and other hill tribes infantry.

II/74a Odenathus' Army 260-271 AD: 1 x General (Odenathus) (4Kn), 2 x cataphracts (4Kn), 1 x Palmyran light horse (LH), 2 x regular archers (4Bw), 2 x archers (3Bw or Ps), 1 x swordsmen (4Bd) or archers (4Bw or Ps) or Roman cavalry (Cv) or Sagittarii indigene horse archers (LH), 2 x Roman legionaries (4Bd), 1 x Roman auxilia (4Ax).

Terrain Type: Dry. **Aggression:** 1. **Enemies** include II/69b Sassanid Persian.

The Palmyran lists cover the period of Palmyran independence. In 260 AD, the Palmyran ruler Odenathus defeated the Sassanids. He was given command of the eastern Roman army by the western emperor Gallienus and so his army includes some Romans.

II/74b Zenobia's Army 271-273 AD: 1 x General Zabdas (4Kn) or Zenobia (Cv or LCm), 2 x cataphracts (4Kn), 1 x cataphracts (4Kn) or swordsmen (4Bd) or archers (3Bw), 2 x Palmyran light horse (LH), 4 x archers (4Bw), 2 x archers (3Bw or Ps).

Terrain Type: Dry. **Aggression:** 1. **Enemies** include II/64b Eastern Roman.

After the murder of Odenathus in 267 AD, his widow Zenobia occupied the Roman provinces of Egypt and Asia Minor and proclaimed her young son emperor in 271 AD. She was defeated by Aurelian's Romans in two epic battles in 272 AD. The list is based on contemporary accounts and archaeological finds from Palmyra and Dura Europos, including the horse armour from Dura and the Dura synagogue fresco, which shows two kinds of light horse (one in blue tunic and red trousers charging with lances and the other horse archers with bow only) as well as swordsmen in hooded mail shirts.

References: *Armies and Enemies of Imperial Rome* P. Barker, *Armies of the Dark Ages* I. Heath, *Roman Histories* Ammianus Marcellinus, *History of the Wars* Procopius, *Maurice's Strategicon* G.T. Dennis (trans), *Warrior of Rome* (series) H. Sidebottom (novels). *Roman Infantry Equipment - The Later Empire* I. P. Stephenson, *Restorer of the World - The Roman Emperor Aurelian J.F. White, Diocletian and the Roman Recovery* S. Williams, *Queen of the East* A. Baron (novel*)* & *Family Favourites* A. Duggan (novel).

Conflict 18: The Romans invade Britain.

When the Emperor Claudius decided to invade Britain in 43AD he started a process which was to continue for the next four hundred years.

II/56 Early Imperial Roman Army 25 BC - 197 AD: 1 x General on horseback (Cv) or on foot (4Bd), 1 x equites (Cv), 4 x legionaries (4Bd), 3 x auxiliary pedites (4Ax), 1 x equites (Cv) or pedites (4Ax) or archers (4Bw or Ps), 1 x Numidians or Moors (LH) or symmachiarii (3Wb) or slingers (Ps) or gladiators (3Bd), 1 x lancers (3Kn) or horse archers (LH) or bolt-shooters (Art) or dromedarii (LCm).

Terrain Type: Arable.   **Aggression**: 3.   **Enemies** include II/53 Ancient British.

The Roman army of this period dates from   from Augustus' reorganisation. This is the period of the legionary equipped with pilum, short gladius sword, semi-cylindrical rectangular shield, iron helmet and lorica segmentata banded iron corslet that is the popular image of the Roman legionary. Auxiliary equites (cavalry) and pedites (infantry) were armed with short spear, javelins and long swords, had more convenient oval shields bearing regimental patterns, wore mail corslets and helmets (initially bronze but quickly replaced by iron). The elephant and camels brought by Claudius when he invaded Britain were too few to be included here and the elements of dromedarii in the list were only used in North Africa.

II/53 Ancient British Army 55 BC - 75 AD: 1 x General in chariot (LCh) or on foot (3Wb), 2 x light horse (LH), 3 x chariots (LCh) or slingers (Ps) or warband (3Wb), 5 x warband (3Wb), 1 x warband (3Wb) or slingers (Ps) or sacrificing druids & screaming women (7Hd).

Terrain Type: Arable. **Aggression**: 0. **Enemies** include II/56 Early Imperial Roman and II/53each other.

Before the arrival of the Romans, the various tribes were independent and frequently at war with one another. One big advantage the Romans had was the ability to make alliances with some of the tribes while they attacked their current enemies – typical "divide and rule".

The British list covers armies of tribes from the area south of the Forth-Clyde line. The prestige arm was the 2 horse, 2 crew light chariotry but the British strength lay in the fierce charges of warbands whose warriors were armed with javelins, long cutting swords and long shields decorated with personalised Celtic patterns. They were clean-shaven except for moustaches, but some washed their hair in lime to produce a sort of white Afro. They wore trousers or knee breeches and usually a shirt worn outside them. Stripes and tartans were popular, but had no clan significance. The tribes of the southwest were especially fond of the sling. The BUA will usually be an Iron-age hill fort.

Famous British war leaders include Caradoc/Caractacus of the Catevellauni who led resistance to the Roman invasion by Claudius 44-50 BC and Boudicca whose Iceni rebels were hindered in defeat by their families in wagons drawn up to watch the battle. Suetonius' invasion of Anglesey was opposed by sacrificing Druids and screaming women.

As time progressed, the tribes allied to Rome found themselves in a difficult position. Rome saw the province of Britannia as conquered and under Roman law. Their allies believed themselves to be independent kingdoms under Celtic law and this could lead to misunderstandings. The most famous of these was the case of Boudicca, widowed queen of the Iceni. Her husband's will left the kingdom divided between the Emperor in Rome and their two daughters. Under Roman law, women could not own property so everything came to the Emperor and this included all Boudicca's own property which under Roman law belonged to her husband. Naturally she objected when the local taxmen came to collect but they had taken the precaution of bringing soldiers with them to police the collection. Boudicca's treatment on this occasion led to a very serious rebellion with three newly built Roman cities destroyed and many civilians killed before Boudicca and her army were defeated.

References: *Armies and Enemies of Imperial Rome* P. Barker, *Histories & Annals* Tacitus, *The Mark of the Horse Lord* R. Sutcliff (novel), *Imperial Governor* G. Shipway (novel), *The Provincial Governor* J. Scott (novel). *The Roman Army at War 100 BC-AD 200* A. Goldsworthy, *The Long Year AD 69* K. Wellesley, *The Roman Legions Recreated in Colour Photographs* D. Peterson, *Year of Four Caesars* H. Nield (novel).

Conflict 19: The Romans Leave Britain.

This period in the fifth and early sixth century covers the change from the Roman province of Britannia to the Anglo-Saxon kingdoms of England. In particular it includes the controversial figure of "King Arthur".

Personally I believe there was a British war-leader called "Arthur" who fought the invading Anglo-Saxons. Everyone (even those who claim that Arthur was entirely mythical) agree that the Anglo-Saxon invasion was not a walk-over. It took them over a hundred years to progress from the first settlements on the east coast to kingdoms controlling the whole of England. This implies serious resistance on the part of the British natives and this in turn implies leaders. All the later legends, however unreliable their details, are unanimous in naming the most successful of these leaders as "Arthur". I doubt our ability at this late date to decide just how much of the legends surrounding Arthur have a factual basis and this will remain controversial, but I see no good reason to doubt his name or existence. Rosemary Sutcliffe's novel "Sword at Sunset" gives a convincing reconstruction of this period.

II/81a Armies of the Dux Britanniorum, the Comes Litoris Saxoni, Britannia Prima, Ambrosius, Riothamus or Arthur 407-470 AD:
1 x General (Cv or 3Kn), 1 x equites or alares (Cv), 1 x equites Dalmatae (LH) or Welsh gentry (Cv), 1 x equites catafractariorum (4Kn) or alares (Cv), 2 x legionari [of VI Victrix or II Augusta] (4Bd) or pedyt (Sp), 5 x cohortales or numeri (4Ax) or pedyt (Sp), 1 x archers (Ps).

Terrain Type: Arable. **Aggression:** 1. **Enemies** include II/73 Anglo-Saxons

The British army list covers the lowland states of mainland Britain. In 406, Roman Britain was cut-off from the central imperial administration in Italy and in 410 the emperor Honorius sent a rescript telling the British local authorities to govern themselves. In doing this, they seem to have evolved into local kingdoms, but historians disagree over the details. The Notitia Dignitatum includes details for the Dux Britanniorum and the Comes Litoris Saxonici and we assume that some of their commands continued after 406 AD. Ambrosius ("last of the Romans") is mentioned as continuing the Roman tradition and it is assumed that Britannia Prima continued in some form. There is also documentary evidence for Riothamus "King of the Britons" who led an army to Gaul in 468 to help against the Visigoths. We assume the army was initially composed of the Roman limitani legiones, old auxiliary alae and cohortes and newer vexillationes and numeri of the garrison troops of the Comes Litoris Saxonici and Dux Britanniarum. These were later replaced by ruler's bodyguards ("comitatus") and town militias, then by infantry levies ("pedyt") and noble cavalry. Near contemporary descriptions are of noble cavalry with yellow crested helmet, mail corselet, javelins, sword and white shield on swift unarmoured horses. Arthur is assumed to be one of the British leaders who fought against the Anglo-Saxon invaders and options for his army are included here.

II/73 Early Anglo-Saxon Armies 428-617 AD: 1 x General (4Wb), 10 x warriors (4Wb), 1 x archers (Ps).

Terrain Type: Arable **Aggression:** 2. **Enemies** include II/81a British armies.

The Anglo-Saxon list covers the Angles and Saxons in Britain from Hengist's arrival in Kent circa 428 as leader of a mercenary force called in by Vortigern, his subsequent rebellion, war against the Romano-British, the establishment of several Angle and Saxon kingdoms in what became England and war between those kingdoms until the accession of Edwin of Northumbria circa 617. All these were light-haired, bearded, wore long-sleeved shirt, trousers and sometimes cloak or cap; and fought with short spear and a moderate-sized round shield. Only nobles had proper swords, the remainder a large knife. Grave goods in burials such as that at Sutton Hoo give an indication of the finery of Anglo-Saxon kings in this period.

References are many and increasing every day. A selection of them includes: *Armies and Enemies of Imperial Rome* P. Barker, *Armies of the Dark Ages* I. Heath, *History of the Kings of Britain* Nennius, *Britannia Prima* R. White, *The Age of Arthur* J. Morris, *The Discovery of King Arthur* G. Ashe, *Civitas to Kingdom* K.R. Dark, *An Age of Tyrants* C.A. Snyder, Lords of Battle S.S. Evans, *The Little Emperors* A. Duggan (novel), *Conscience of the King* A. Duggan (novel), *The Badon Parchments* J. Masefield (novel), *Artorius Rex* J. Gloag (novel), *Men Went to Cattraeth* J. James (novel), *Sword at Sunset* Rosemary Sutcliffe (novel).

Conflict 20: Attila's Huns (in memory of Bob O'Brien)

Bob O'Brien was one of the original members of WRG and is remembered for his "Hordes of Horrible Hairy Hunnic Horse-archers".

II/80a Attila's army 433-453 AD: 1 x General (Cv or LH), 5 x Hun horse archers (LH), 1 x Ostrogoths and Gepids (3Kn), 2 x Hun horse archers (LH) or Burgundian, Rugian, Thuringian and Frankish subject warriors (4Wb), 2 x subject warriors (4Wb), 1 x archers (Ps).

Terrain Type: Steppe. **Aggression:** 4. **Enemies** include II/67b Goths, II/69b Sassanids, II/72d, II/82b Eastern Patrician Romans

----

II/80d Other Hunnic Armies 374-558 AD: 1 x General (Cv or LH), 11 x horse archers (LH).

Terrain Type: Steppe. **Aggression:** 3. **Enemies** include, II/67b Goths, II/69b Sassanids, II/72a, II/82b Eastern Patrician Romans

The Hunnic lists cover western Hunnic armies from their emergence from the steppes in around 374 BC. Contemporaries stress the Huns' savagery and barbarism, saying that "while other peoples were carried on horseback, the Huns lived there". Huns are described as wearing animal-skin garments and "furrowing their cheeks with knives to prevent the growth of beards". Their mounts were big, tractable, tough, but ugly horses with heavy heads and flat rumps. Only a few nobles had armour and lances. Others accompanied bows with bone-tipped javelins or lasso. The western Huns were most dangerous when united, for example the army of Attila.

II/67b Gothic Armies 200-493 AD: 1 x General (3Kn), 5 x noble cavalry (3Kn), 6 x javelinmen if Heruls, archers if not (Ps).

Terrain Type: Littoral if Heruls, Arable if not. **Aggression**: 3. **Enemies** include II/80a and II/80d Huns

The Gothic list covers the Greuthingi/Greutungi Goths ("men of the steppes") from their arrival in the Ukraine. They did not use long lances or stirrups. Gothic archers feared cavalry. Heruls from by the Sea of Azov had good light infantry, but said to be drunken and treacherous. They lacked metal armour or helmets.

II/69b Sassanid Persian Army 225-493 AD: 1 x General (Cv), 1 x cataphracts (4Kn), 4 x asavaran (Cv), 1 x elephants (El) or asavaran

(Cv), 1 x asavaran (Cv) or nomad or vassal horse archers (LH), 1 x asavaran (Cv) or archers and slingers (Ps), 1 x nomad or vassal horse archers (LH) or Arabs (LH) or Dailami (4Ax) or other hillmen (3Ax), 2 x levies (7Hd).

Terrain Type: Arable. **Aggression:** 3. **Enemies** include II/82b Eastern Patrician Romans, II/80a and II/80d (Huns)

A limited number of Parthian style cataphracts (4Kn) provided a striking force of lancers in full metal armour riding metal-armoured horses but the strength of the army was the asavaran who wore mail shirts, rode horses in full leather or felt protection and were armed with bow and heavy sword. Peasant levy spearmen with rectangular shields were brought for camp labour, but formed a rear line in battle. War elephants are first attested in 337. They were not used to fight cavalry, but only positioned behind the infantry or to head desperate assaults. Vassal nations provided horse archers and Dailami and other hill tribes mercenary infantry.

II/82b Eastern Patrician Roman Army 408-493 AD: 1 x General (3Kn), 1 x equites (3Kn or Cv), 2 x horse archers (LH), 1 x equites clibanarii (4Kn) or Gothic foederati (3Kn), 2 x legionaries (4Bd), 2 x auxilia palatina (4Ax), 2 x legionaries (4Bd) or German foederati (4Wb) or archers (Ps) or Isaurian javelinmen (Ps), 1 x archers (Ps or 4Bw).

Terrain Type: Arable. **Aggression:** 1. **Enemies** include II/69b Sassanid, II/80a and II/80d Huns

The Patrician Roman list runs from the murder of Stilicho 408AD. Regular Late Roman units continued in existence, but service in the legions had become unpopular while the survivors of the Gothic foederati enlisted as individuals under Roman discipline. The loss of territory in the west damaged recruitment; and the gap was increasingly filled by barbarian groups enlisted under their own leaders as foederati who fought in their own native style.

References: *Armies and Enemies of Imperial Rome* P. Barker, *The World of the Huns* O.J. Maenchen-Helfen, *The Death of Attila* C.Holland (novel), *The Year of the Horsetails* R.F. Tapsell (novel). *Goths and Romans 332-489* P. Heather. *Armies of the Dark Ages* I. Heath, *Emperor Prefects & Kings* P.S. Barnwell. *The Rise and Decline of the Late Roman Field Army* R. Cromwell, *Warfare in Roman Europe AD 350-425* H. Elton, *The Fall of the West* A. Goldsworthy, *The Rome That Did Not Fall* S. Williams & G. Friell.

Conflict 21: Christian Nubian vs Arab Conquest

With the conversion of the Nobades to Monophysite Christianity around 550 AD, three Christian kingdoms arose in the Sudan, namely Nobatia, Makouria and Alwa. After Nobatia was conquered by Makouria circa 700, the combined state was called Nubia. It fought successive Muslim Egyptian regimes and inflicted the first serious reverse on the Muslim Arab conquest armies at Dongola in 643, but also enjoyed periods of trade with Egypt.

III/12 Christian Nubian Army: 1 x General and court cavalry (Cv or 3Kn), 2 x camel warriors (Cm), 2 x light horse (LH), 3 x warriors (4Bd/4Ax), 3 x archers (3/4Bw), 1 x levies (7Hd) or Arab archers (Ps) or Arab camel riders (LCm).

Terrain Type: Dry. **Aggression: 1. Enemies** include III/12 each other and III/25b Arab Conquest

The army was renowned for its foot archers. Contemporary depictions of other foot show segmented nasal-guard helmet, quilted armour, cloak, a figure-of-eight shield, a spear and a broad-bladed shafted stabbing weapon similar to the later Zulu assegai. Since most inhabitants were poor peasants, these well-armed foot were probably an elite standing army. Mounted troops used both horses and camels throughout the period and it was one of the few army to use charging camelry. Court nobility probably provided the cavalry in gold-embroidered robes seen in Nubian art.

III/25b Arab Conquest Army 639-660 AD: 1 x General (Cv), 4 x "jund" regular cavalry (Cv), 1 x Muslim archers (3/4Bw), 5 x Muslim swordsmen (4Bd), 1 x javelinmen (3Ax) or javelinmen and slingers (Ps) or camel scouts (LCm).

Terrain Type: Dry. **Aggression**: 4. **Enemies** include III/12 Christian Nubians.

This list covers the wars of the Prophet and his immediate successors from the "hijra" or migration of the Prophet and his followers to Medina until the establishment of the Umayyad Khalifate by Mu'awiya. Many horses were acquired in the initial conquests. This aim of conquering the whole area inevitably brought them into conflict with the Christian kingdoms of the Sudan.

References: *Armies of the Dark Ages* I. Heath, *The Great Arab Conquests* J.B. Glubb, *The Great Arab Conquests* H. Kennedy.

Conflict 22: Early (pre-Samurai) Japan.

The Japanese list covers the army of the Kofun state that preceded the rise of the Samurai.

III/7a Kofun Army 500-645 AD: 1 x General on horseback (Cv) or on foot (4Bw), 1 x armoured horse archers (Cv), 2 x uji noble archers with armour and pavise (4Bw), 4 x less-armoured retainers (3/4Bw), 2 x uji with long spear and pavise (Sp/4Pk), 1 x Emishi scout archers (Ps) or levies (7Hd), 1 x levy archers (3Bw) or levies (7Hd).

Terrain Type: Hilly. **Aggression**: 2. **Enemies** include III/6a Emishi.

Kofun armies intervened in Korea or fought the wild Emishi of northern Japan. Initially the army were mainly provided by uji nobles and their retainers. Most were armoured archers who shot from behind a line of portable pavises, but some others instead fought with spears up to 14 feet long. Armoured cavalry had been copied from Korea, but with weaker horses and lacking lances. Horse armour had been abandoned by the start of this list.

III/6a Emishi Army 500-699 AD: 1 x General (3/4Bw), 11 x archers (Ps or 3Bw).

Terrain Type: Forest. **Aggression**: 0. **Enemy**: III/7a Japanese

The Emishi were the indigenous people of northern Japan, including both the Ainu and groups ethnically closer to the Japanese. They are doubtfully credited with introducing curved swords and leather armour to the Japanese. In the sixth and seventh centuries they were described as archers. "They swarm like ants and gather like bees! When we attack, they flee! When we relax, they assault our fortifications!" Ainu are described as "blood-drinking" hunters rather than farmers, tattooed, wearing fur garments (often concealing swords) and carrying arrows for their short bows in the topknot of their hair.

References: *Heavenly Warriors* W.W. Farris, *The History of Japanese Armor (Volume 1) - From the Yayoi period to the Muromachi period* R. Nakanishi, *Slingshot* 251 & 252.

Conflict 23: Maurikian Byzantine vs Avars & Bulgars

This list covers the period from the appointment of the future emperor Maurikios (Maurice) as Comes Excubitorum or Foederatorum and his reforms of the army and it is largely based on his surviving manual.

III/17 Maurikian Byzantine Army 575 AD - 650 AD: 1 x General (Cv/6Cv), 5 x kavallarioi (6Cv/Cv), 3 x cursores (LH) or skoutatoi (Sp), 2 x cursores (LH) or foot archers (4Bw or Ps), 1 x optimates (3Kn) or javelinmen (Ps) or bolt-shooters (Art).

Terrain Type: Arable. **Aggression**: 1. **Enemies** include III/13a and III/13b Avars and III/14a Bulgars.

The army was now almost entirely regular. Kavallarioi were deployed in two separated lines an arrow shot apart with the commanding general in the second. They wore helmets with small plumes, hooded mail shirts extending to the elbows and knees, large cloaks, tunic, trousers and boots. They rode on saddles with stirrups copied from the Avars and the horses of the front rank wore frontal armour of iron or felt. They formed up to 10 ranks deep, the 2 foremost and the last armed with long Avar lance, sword and kite-shaped shield, the others only with bow and sword. Some of the bow-armed could instead form on the flanks of the lancers (which were then called "defensores") or be sent out in front as "cursores" or to scout. Optimates were noble foreigners fighting with their native weapons. If infantry were used, their units usually alternated with kavallarioi or formed the centre. They wore knee-length gothic tunics, a simple cloak and shoes, and short hair. Most were skoutatoi with a moderate-length spear, helmet, big shield painted a regimental colour, sword, sling and lead-weighted darts. Those in front had mail corslets. Archers formed behind the skoutatoi, but if they were plentiful they deployed on the flanks. In bad going, they joined the javelinmen to skirmish, javelinmen being preferred in woods. Both had a small round shield and a short axe. Bolt-shooters were in swivel mounts on carts.

III/13a Avar Army 632-826 AD: 1 x General (Cv), 9 x noble cavalry (Cv), 2 x cavalry (LH or Cv).

Terrain Type: Steppe. **Aggression**: 3. **Enemies** include III/17 Byzantines

III/13b Avar Army 558-631 AD: 1 x General (Cv), 4 x nobles (Cv), 2 x horse archers (LH), 3 x Slav javelinmen (3Ax), 1 x Slav archers & scouts (Ps), 1 x Slav javelinmen (3Ax) or [in 626 AD only] stone-throwers (Art).

Terrain Type: Steppe. **Aggression**:3. **Enemies** include III/17 Byzantines

The Avars were probably the combined remnants of the Juan-juan and the White Huns after both were driven west by the Gok Turks. They subjugated the Bulgars, the Gepids and many of the southern Slavs and in 562 came into conflict with the Frankish kingdoms, but lost face after a failed attack on Constantinople in 626 in conjunction with the Sassanids. This inspired the Slavs and Bulgars to rebel, leaving only a rump Avar state in modern Hungary. The Franks led by Charlemagne inflicted several defeats on them. They were finished off by Bulgars in 826. Maurice describes Avar cavalry as having mail, swords (but not shields), bows and lances (slung over their shoulders when not in use); and the richest as riding horses with frontal armour of iron or felt. They probably introduced the stirrup to the Byzantines. He says that they were fond of deceit and surprise and fought with multiple groups in a single wide line with a small reserve.

III/14a Bulgar Army 558-674 AD: 1 x General (Cv), 5 x boyars (Cv) or horse archers (LH), 6 x horse archers (LH).

Terrain Type: Steppe. **Aggression**: 1. **Enemies** include III/17 Byzantines

The Bulgars originated as a combination of Utigur and Kutrigur Hun remnants with Sabirs and Onogur. They became subject to the Avars in 558 but cast off Avar rule in 631 and formed the new united khanate of Great Bulgaria around the Sea of Azov. After defeat by the Khazars around 675, some fled up the river Volga and formed the "Volga Bulgar" state. Most fled to the Danube basin where they founded an empire rivalling the Byzantines that lasted until 1018. Their greatest King was King Krum 807-814. Cavalry are depicted in one Byzantine manuscript with small round shields and lances and wearing trousers vertically striped in red, white and blue.

References: *Armies & Enemies of Imperial Rome* P. Barker, *Armies of the Dark Ages* I. Heath, *Maurice's Strategikon* G.T. Dennis (trans), *The Age of Hippotoxotai* I. Syvanne, *The Byzantine Wars* J. Haldon, *Warfare, State and Society in the Byzantine World 565-1204* John Haldon.

Conflict 24: Ancient Burma and their enemies

This list covers the Burmese army from the foundation of the kingdom of Pyu (circa 500) until King Tabinshweti of Toungoo's campaigns of re-unification. Before the unification of Burma in 1044 by King Anawrahta, the army was mainly infantry with few elephants, but he shifted the emphasis to massed elephants.

III/9a Burmese Army 500-1043 AD: 1 x General (El), 1 x cavalry (Cv), 6 x spearmen (3Ax), 3 x archers or crossbowmen (3Bw or 3Cb), 1 x archers (3Bw or 3Cb or Ps).

Terrain Type: Tropical. **Aggression:** 2. **Enemies** III/9a each other.

III/9b Burmese Army 1044-1526 AD: 1 x General on elephant (El) or on dragon horse (Cv), 2 x elephants with large crew or escorts (El), 1 x cavalry (Cv), 3 x spearmen (3Ax), 1 x spearmen (3Ax) or guards (3Bd), 1 x guards (4Cb), 2 x crossbowmen or archers (3Cb or 3Bw), 1 x archers (3Bw or 3Cb or Ps) or Thai spearmen (3Wb).

Terrain Type: Tropical. **Aggression:** 2. **Enemies** include III/9b each other and III/10c Hindu Indians

Contemporary sources describe Burmese elephant crew as 12-16 or 8-10, but it has been suggested that only 4 rode in a howdah while the rest walked alongside. Kings rode a white elephant with a gold chain ornamented with precious stones around its neck and some battles were decided by personal combat. Cavalry were recruited from the Shan, who occupied the only extensive grass lands in Burma. They were shield-less, wore quilted armour and had black or white bull's hair at the heads of their spears. Some generals led raids on horses disguised as dragons. Guard infantry wore gilt helmets and quilted black cotton jackets and fought with sword and shield. Other foot were more numerous than efficient. Archers could have either bows or crossbows, but were out-shot by dismounted Mongols. The standard tactic was a mass charge by elephants in the centre, possibly supported by foot, with foot guards in a second line protecting the general and cavalry supported by foot trying to outflank.

III/10b Rajput Army 747-1300 AD: 1 x General on elephant (El) or on horseback (3Kn), 2 x cavalry (3Kn), 1 x elephants (El) or cavalry (3Kn), 2 x swordsmen (3Bd), 3 x archers (3Bw), 1 x camel riders (Cm) or archers (3Bw), 1 x javelinmen (Ps), 1 x javelinmen (Ps) or camp followers (7Hd).

Terrain Type: Dry or Tropical. **Aggression:** 2. **Enemies** include III/10b each other, III/10c Hindu Indian and III/38 Arab Indian

III/10c Other Hindu Indian Armies 545-1510 AD: 1 x General (El), 1 x elephants (El), 2 x cavalry (Cv), 1 x swordsmen (3Bd), 4 x archers (3Bw), 1 x javelinmen (Ps), 1 x javelinmen (Ps) or camp followers (7Hd), 1 x elephants (El) or (if Vijayanagar after 1336) rocketeers or bombards (Art).

Terrain Type: Tropical. **Aggression:** 2. **Enemies** include III/9b Burmese, III/10b & III/10c each other and III/38 Arab Indian

The Indian lists cover the Hindu states of northern and central India from the fall of the Gupta empire until the introduction of hand firearms. The Guptas were replaced by a number of small states. These were all attacked by a new wave of Turkish Muslim invaders that in 1206 became the Sultanate of Delhi and conquered all of them except the southern state of Vijayanagar.

The Rajputs were a warrior caste, thought to be descended from Saka or Huna (Hephthalites), who ruled states in central and western India and fought both against and for the Sultanate. They had a strong heroic ethos and ended lost battles with a suicidal charge instead of surrender and wore yellow as a badge of fanaticism. Elephants were described as armoured and carrying howdahs containing several crew. Cavalry were armed with bow, sword and shield, were armoured and sometimes rode barded horses. Foot were unarmoured and skimpily dressed. Swordsmen had a small round shield.

III/38 Arab Indian Army 751-1206 AD: 1 x General (Cv), 3 x Arab & Sindi cavalry (Cv), 2 x Arab spearmen (Sp), 2 x Arab archers (3/4Bw or Ps), 2 x Hindu archers (3Bw), 1 x Hindu archers (3Bw) or javelinmen (Ps), 1 x Hindu swordsmen (3Bd) or archers (3Bw).

Terrain Type: Tropical. **Aggression:** 3. **Enemies** include III/10b and III/10c Hindu Indians.

Between 710 and 833, Arab forces penetrated the River Indus from the sea and conquered most of the regions of Sind and Kutch before being defeated by the Hindu Pratiharas, after which it survived as the two small states of Mansurah and Multan.

References: *Armies of Medieval Burma AD700-1300* D. Mersey, *Armies of the Middle Ages Vol.2* I. Heath, Slingshot 248.

Conflict 25: Maya & Toltecs in Mesoamerica.

We know of no single Maya state, only rival cities which fought among themselves. After around 987, they were conquered by the Toltecs.

III/22b Maya Army 988-1282 AD: 1 x General with Ah Camul mercenary bodyguard (4Bd), 1 x Toltec or Itza nobles (4Bd), 9 x Maya warriors (3Ax), 1 x peasant slingers (Ps).

Terrain Type: Tropical. **Aggression:** 0. **Enemies:** III/22b each other and III/59 Toltecs

Mayan warriors were described as ugly, tattooed, wearing a loin cloth and armed with a short spear, a club and a rectangular shield that rolled-up like a window blind. Leaders of Mayan descent added jaguar hide or quilted cotton armour and wooden or hide helmets with elaborate feather crests. Toltec and Itza leaders and Ah Camul mercenaries also wore cotton armour, but fought with an obsidian bladed maquahuitl, javelins thrown with an atlatl and a small round shield.

III/59 Toltec Army 930 AD - 1168 AD: 1 x General (4Bd), 10 x warriors (4Bd), 1 x warriors (4Bd) or peasant slingers (Ps).

Terrain Type: Arable. **Aggression:** 2. **Enemies** include III/22b Mayas and III/59 each other.

The Toltecs started as one of the early waves of "Dog People" barbarian immigrants into Mexico from the north and their leader Mixcoatl "Cloud Serpent" established a capital at Culhuacan in 930. His son Quetzalcoatl "Plumed Serpent" moved to Tula around 968 and made it the capital of a large civilised empire, but was forced out by his rival Tezcatlipoca. The leader of the Toltec immigrants that imposed their rule on the Maya was called Kukulcan, which also means "Plumed Serpent". Toltec art is obsessed with depictions of ugly-looking warriors with pillbox hats, wooden swords edged with obsidian volcanic glass called maquahuitl, atlatl dart-throwers and small shields. There is no specific evidence of mercenary or other skirmishers, but the usual peasant slingers of the area cannot be discounted.

References: *Armies of the 16th Century Vol 2.* I. Heath, *Slingshot 107. War and Society in Ancient Mesoamerica* R. Hassig.

Conflict 26: Alfred the Great against the Danes.

The Anglo-Saxon kingdoms of Wessex, Mercia, East Anglia and Northumbria and other minor states remained independent and frequently at war with each other. This continued until the arrival of the Danes and the wars of Alfred of Wessex 871-899 and others.

III/24b Middle Anglo-Saxon Army 701-1016: 1 x General (Alfred) (4Bd), 2 x hird (4Bd), 6 x select fyrd (Sp), 2 x select fyrd (Sp) or great fyrd (7Hd), 1 x archers or scouts (Ps).

Terrain Type: Arable. **Aggression:** 2. **Enemies** include III/24b each other and III/40b Danes.

Hird were thanes and elite followers who wore helmets and mail and owned swords as well as spears. Select fyrd were the best of the spear-armed remainder. A considerable increase in shield diameter around 700 is taken as evidence of a switch to shield-wall tactics. A boy was given a shield and spear on his twelfth birthday, then took his place in the rear ranks unless used to guard the baggage.

III/40b Viking Army 850-1280 AD: 1 x General and huscarls (4Bd), 10 x hird (4Bd), 1 x archers (Ps or 4Bw) or berserks (3Wb).

Terrain Type: Littoral. **Aggression**: 4. **Enemies** include III/24b Anglo-Saxon and III/40b each other.

The Danish or Viking list covers Norse armies from the first Viking raids on Britain until the establishment of the feudal system in their homeland. Most warriors are classed as Blades because of the universal ownership of swords and axes and the stress placed on individual weapon skills. There were also a small number of slightly insane berserks. Huscarls are taken to be the most skilled and armoured men, nobles and their professional followers. Hird were the mass of the army. They are assumed to have less skill and mail than huscarles. Archers were usually used onboard ship or as skirmishers.

References: *Armies of the Dark Ages* I. Heath, *The Early Wars of Wessex* A. Major, *Anglo-Saxon Weapons and Warfare* R. Underwood, *Kings and Kingdoms of Early Anglo-Saxon England* B. Yorke, *An Alternative History of Britain: The Anglo-Saxon Age* T. Venning, *Armies of Feudal Europe* I. Heath, *The Viking Art of War* P. Griffith, *The Long Ships* F. Bengtsson (novel), *The King of Athelney* A. Duggan (novel).

Conflict 27: Fighting the Moors in Spain

In their attempt to conquer the world, the Muslims spread along North Africa and into Spain. They made some attempts to extend into France but for much of the time the Pyrenees formed a barrier between the Muslim lands and Christendom. In 778 AD, Charlemagne took an army south into Spain in an attempt to reconquer some of the lands of the Roman empire taken by the "Moors" or "Saracens" (as these Muslims were now called). He was not very successful and as he returned home through the pass of Roncevalles, his rearguard was ambushed, probably by local bandits, and most of them were slain. From this minor incident, we have the "Song of Roland", an epic poem about heroes fighting against the Moors. The Carolingian army is described here. Swabian and Bavarian caballarii fought better on foot. Whether the select levy fought with sword and big shield before Charlemagne is disputed.

III/28 Carolingian Frankish Army 639-888 AD: 1 x General (3Kn), 2 x caballarii (3Kn), 2 x Swabian or Bavarian caballarii (3Kn//4Bd) or [1 x Basque or Gascon javelinmen (Ps) + 1 x Andalusian, Basque or Gascon javelin-throwing light horse (LH)], 1 x caballarii (3Kn) or if Thuringians (Cv), 4 x select levies (all 4Bd or all Sp until 814, then all Sp), 1 x archers (3Bw or Ps), 1 x archers (Ps) or lantwer lesser levies (7Hd).

Terrain Type: Arable. **Aggression:** 3. **Enemies** include III/33 Early Muslims and III/34b Andalusians.

The Song of Roland is an epic tale of bravery and betrayal in an endless war against the "Saracens". In the song, Charlemagne has conquered most of Spain and makes a truce with the last Saracen King, but is betrayed by Count Guenes who incites the Saracens to attack the retreating French Army. Charlemagne is returning to France with his main army when the rearguard, led by Roland, his friend Oliver and Archbishop Turpin is attacked by a vast horde of Saracens. Roland is begged to sound his horn and recall the rest of the army to help, but at first he refuses, preferring to trust to his own prowess with his sword Durandel. When he does sound the horn, Charlemagne and the army return but are too late to save them.

III/33 Early Muslim Army 696-1160 AD: 1 x General (Cv), 1 x Arab or Berber lancers or Khurasanians (Cv), 3 x Berber javelin-throwing light horse (LH), 3 x Berber javelinmen (Ps/3Ax) or Arab, Berber or black slave spearmen (Sp), 1 x Arab archers (3/4Bw or Ps) or Berber archers or slingers (Ps), 3 x Berber javelinmen (Ps).

Terrain Type: Littoral. **Aggression:** 1. **Enemies** III/28 Carolingian Franks, III/33 each other and III/34b Andalusians.

These armies were a combination of coastal and city-dwelling Arabs with Berber converts from the hinterland and slave troops brought across the Sahara. They would have fought Charlemagne in 778 and could also have fought our second hero, El Cid.

For the second of our heroes, we have to move forward to the eleventh century. Rodrigo or Riy Diaz was a Castilian noble born in Burgos in 1040. By this time the original Muslim states set up in Spain "Al-Andalus" had fragmented into warring Berber and Andalusian Arab emirates and revanchist Christian kingdoms. Rodrigo, known as El Cid took part in the war between the two brothers Sancho II and Alfonso VI in Castile. Later El Cid was banished from Castile and took service with the Moorish King of Saragossa for a while. Finally he took control of Valencia where he ruled as king in all but name until his death in 1099.

III/34b Andalusian Army 766-1172 AD: 1 x General (Cv), 1 x ghulam or Andalusian cavalry (Cv), 2 x mujahids (LH), 1 x Christian guard (3Kn or 4Cb) or black guard (Sp), 2 x archers or slingers (Ps), 2 x Andalusian or black spearmen (Sp), 3 x Berber javelinmen (Ps).

Terrain Type: Arable. **Aggression**: 1. **Enemies** include : III/28 Carolingian Franks, III/33 Early Muslims and III/34b each other.

Both El Cid and his enemies would probably have led Andalusian armies but may have met a Muslim army. The original invasion force consisted of a small number of Arab cavalry and masses of Berber foot, but was reinforced by regular cavalry of the jund from Syria and developed into the army listed above. The jund regular organisation was continued by the Umayyads, but reliance on them came to be replaced by non-Arab speakers called "the Silent Ones". Cavalry were usually Frankish, Lombard and Spanish professionals but were misleadingly referred to as "Slav ghulams". They were supplemented by unpaid irregulars serving for loot called "mujahids". Berber horse, negro foot and even Christian knights were employed as mercenaries.

References: *Armies of the Dark Ages* I. Heath, Slingshot 273, 274, 276, 279, 280, 294 *Armies of Feudal Europe* I. Heath.

Conflict 28: Battle of Hastings in 1066.

Harold Godwinson became King of England following the death of Edward the Confessor. He was challenged, Harold Hardrarda's Vikings and then by William of Normandy. One challenge he could deal with, but two in quick succession proved too much.

III/72 Harold's Anglo-Saxon Army 1066 AD: 1 x General (4Bd), 2 x huscarls (4Bd), 4 x select fyrd (Sp), 4 x great fyrd (Sp/7Hd), 1 x archers and slingers (Ps) or select fyrd (Sp).

Terrain Type: Arable. **Aggression:** 1. **Enemies** include III/52 Normans and III/40b Vikings.

The huscarls were professional royal bodyguards wearing acorn-shaped helmets and long mail shirts, having long kite-shaped shields and fighting with long axes swung two-handed. The select fyrd were nobles, thanes and their best equipped followers, often similarly armoured but fighting with spear and sword and shield. Great fyrd were the remaining levies, mostly unarmoured and less rigidly under control, so best simulated by 7Hd. At Hastings they pursued rashly off their hill.

III/40b Harold Hardarda's Viking Army 1066 AD: 1 x General and huscarls (4Bd), 10 x hird (4Bd), 1 x archers (Ps or 4Bw) or berserks (3Wb).

Terrain Type: Littoral. **Aggression**: 4. **Enemies** include III/24b Anglo-Saxon and III/40b each other.

Harold Hardarda led a Viking army. Most of his warriors are classed as Blades because of the universal ownership of swords and axes and the stress placed on individual weapon skills. The huscarls are taken to be the most skilled and uniformly armoured men and the hird were the mass of the army. Bows mainly used on ship-board, although archers could occasionally be sent out to skirmish.

III/52 William's Norman Army 1066 AD: 1 x General (William) (3Kn), 3 x milites (3Kn), 3 x milites (3Kn or 4Bd), 2 x milites (3Kn or if Bretons Cv), 2 x archers (3Bw) or spearmen (Sp), 1 x archers (3Bw/Ps) or crossbowmen (3Cb/Ps) or servants, grooms and peasants (7Hd) or Gascon javelinmen (Ps or LH).

Terrain Type: Arable. **Aggression:** 3 Norman. **Enemies** include III/40b Vikings and III/72 Anglo-Saxons.

William led a Norman army. "Milites" was the contemporary name for the upper-class horseman familiar from the Bayeux tapestry and who would soon be termed "knights". When invading England in 1066, many of the milites could not be accompanied by horses.

References: *Armies of the Dark Ages* I. Heath, *The Battle of Hastings* S. Morillo (which includes monochrome illustrations of the Bayeux tapestry), *An Alternative History of Britain: The Anglo-Saxon Age* T. Venning, *The Cunning of the Dove* A. Duggan (novel), *Armies of Feudal Europe* I. Heath, *Warfare under the Anglo-Norman Kings 1066-1135* S. Morillo, *Anglo-Norman Warfare* M. Strickland (Ed), *The Viking Art of War* P. Griffith, *The Long Ships* F. Bengtsson (novel). www.bayeauxtapestry.org.uk for coloured images of the tapestry.

Conflict 29: Early Crusades in Syria

I first met the Crusades as a teenager when I bought and read a copy of Sir Walter Scott's novel "The Talisman". I now know the novel to be wildly inaccurate and improbable in many of its details and set in a later Crusade, but the inspiration and atmosphere has stayed with me as I moved on to more reliable sources. Once again the importance of the initial inspiration is the fact that it led me to discover more about the period.

IV/7 Early Crusader army1096 AD - 1128 AD: 1 x General (3Kn), 3 x knights (3Kn or 4Bd), 4 x spearmen (Sp or 7Hd), 2 x crossbowmen (4Cb), 1 x archers (3Bw), 1 x pilgrims (5Hd or 7Hd) or Byzantine tourkopouloi horse archers (LH).

Terrain Type: Arable.   **Aggression:** 4 until 1100 AD, then 1. **Enemies** include IV/6a & IV/6c Syrians.

This list covers Crusader armies from the arrival at Constantinople of the 1st Crusade until the formation of the military orders. It includes the taking of Antioch and Jerusalem; the establishment of the Kingdom of Jerusalem, the Principality of Antioch and the Counties of Edessa and Tripoli; and then the initial defense of the Kingdom against the Fatimids and failed Crusader attempts to capture Aleppo and Damascus. Although able to charge through most enemy cavalry, Crusader knights were vulnerable to being surrounded and picked off in detail by horse archers if they charged too rashly. In the latter part of the First Crusade, severe losses of horses due to lack of forage forced many knights to fight on foot. A small Byzantine contingent under Tatikios accompanied the army as far as Antioch. The fiercely charging Norman and French knights that provided the army with its punch now wore mail hauberks extending to the wrist and the richer ones that fought in the front rank had mail trousers. Long kite shields and acorn helmets were still in use, but not yet closed helmets, heraldic shield emblems and horse caparisons. The pilgrims providing the foot included some effective crossbowmen.

IV/6a Turkish-ruled Syrian states 1092-1286 AD: 1 x General with ghulams (Cv), 3 x Syrian or Kurdish cavalry (Cv), 2 x Turkoman horse archers (LH), 2 x Turkoman horse archers or Bedouin (LH), 1 x ghulams (Cv) or ghazi (3Wb), 1 x Ahdath militia (7Hd), 1 x archers (Ps), 1 x archers (Ps) or javelinmen (3Ax) or mutatawwi'a (5Hd).

Terrain Type: Arable. **Aggression:** 1. **Enemies** include   IV/7 Crusaders.

IV/6c Arab dynasties 1092-1172 AD: 1 x General (Cv), 3 x Syrian cavalry (Cv), 2 x Bedouin (LH), 1 x ghazis (3Wb), 2 x Ahdath militia (7Hd), 1 x archers (Ps), 2 x archers (Ps) or mutatawwi'a (5Hd).

Terrain Type: Arable. **Aggression:** 1. Enemies include IV/7 Crusaders.

These lists cover the Muslim armies of Syria. The rulers of Syrian cities became semi-independent and the most important were the Turkish rulers of Damascus and Aleppo. Antioch and Jerusalem also had Turkish rulers, but fell during the first Crusade to the Crusaders; and later to the Fatimids. The smaller Syrian cities of Hama, Homs, Tripoli and Shaizar were ruled until the Zankid conquest by Arab dynasties. The Ahdath were the local citizen militia or irregular police who played a large part in fighting the Crusaders in Syria.

The list also covers the armies of Mosul from Zanki's acquisition of Aleppo in 1128. He took Edessa in 1145, then sent his Kurdish general Shirkuh to conquer Egypt. The list then covers local Ayyubid dynasties in Syria from Saladin's death in 1103 until the Mamkuks absorbed Kerak in 1286. Ghazi were inspired by religion, mutatawwi'a by loot. Syrian armoured cavalry were armed with lance, sword and shield, but no bow, but rulers could supplement them with ghulam slave troops armed with bow, sword or mace and shield, but not always with lance or spear.

References: *Armies and Enemies of the Crusades* I. Heath, *Victory in the East* J. France, *Knight with Armour* A. Duggan (novel), *Count Bohemond* A. Duggan (novel).

Conflict 30: Horse Archers in the Desert.

The Tuareg list covers the face-veiled and indigo-clad camel-riding nomads from deep in the Sahara desert. They mainly fought each other, but also intervened in the western Sudan.

III/70 Tuareg Army 1000-1880 AF 1 x General (Cm), 3 x Ihaggeren and Imrad camel warriors (Cm), 2 x camel warriors (Cm) or Iklan (Ps), 5 x camel warriors (Cm) or mountain tribesmen (3Wb), 1 x scouts (LCm) or mountain tribes slingers (Ps).

Terrain Type: Dry. **Aggression**: 1. **Enemies** include III/69 Western Sudanese and III/70 each other.

Tuareg riding camels are pale cream in colour, darker animals being used only for baggage. The Ihaggeren aristocrats raided, armed with the short all-iron "allarh" lance, a long straight sword and a long white hide shield, Imrad vassals without shields but with allarh or a quiver of javelins herded goats and camels and Iklan negro serfs were armed with javelins and daggers.

III/69 Western Sudanese Army 1000-1591 AD: 1 x General (4Kn or Cv or 4Bd), 1 x yan lifida (4Kn) or yan kwarbai (Cv) or yam asigiri (Sp) or pathfinders (LCm), 2 x yan kwarbai (Cv or LH), [1 x yam lifida baka (4Bw) or yam baka (3Bw) + 5 x yam baka (3Bw)] or 6 x Kanembu (Sp), 2 x yam fate-fate (4Bd) or yam assigiri (Sp) or yam mashi (3Ax) or yam baka (Ps/3Bw) or Zagi (Ps).

Terrain Type: Steppe. **Aggression**: 0. **Enemies** include III/69 each other and III/70 Tuareg

The western Sudan is the lightly wooded rolling grassland south of the Sahara desert. The general's bodyguard were protected against local archery and javelins by thick quilted armour for man and horse introduced about 1390. Yan kwarbai were lesser javelin cavalry, some tribes using armour, others relying entirely on speed. The main infantry types were: Yam baka who used weak bows to shoot dense clouds of un-flighted poisoned arrows, yam fate-fate who used long straight sword and shield, Kanembu who were spearmen with very large shields whoadvanced slowly in close formation and Zagi who were unshielded javelinmen that often supported yan kwarbai.

References: *Warfare in the Sokoto Caliphate* J.P. Smaldone, *Slingshot 216, 217, 221 & 224, African Arms & Armour* C. Spring, *Warfare in Atlantic Africa 1500-1800* J.K. Thornton.

Conflict 31: The Ottomans establish their empire.

The Ottomans, under Othman 1, established their empire in the latter fourteenth century. Among the enemies they had to conquer were the Persians.

IV/55a Ottoman army 1281-1361 AD: 1 x General with sipahis (Cv), 1 x feudal sipahis (Cv), 7 x ghazi horse archers (LH), 1 x spearmen (3Ax or Sp) or levendat (7Hd) or ghazis (LH), 2 x azabs with javelin, bow or sling (Ps).

Terrain Type: Arable. **Aggression**: 4. **Enemies** include IV/42 Persians.

The Ottoman list covers Turkish armies from the accession of Othman I until that of Selim I. Early Ottoman armies depended on ghazi religious fanatics, plus levendat policing conquered territory. These were replaced by sipahi with bow (a few also with lance) on timariot land grants and by akinji borderers fighting for loot. Azabs with javelin, bow or sling were recruited for each campaign.

IV/42 Islamic Persian Army 1245 AD - 1393 AD: 1 x General (Cv), 1 x lance and bow cavalry (Cv), 2 x bow-only cavalry (Cv), 4 x bow-only cavalry (Cv), 1 x Turcoman horse archers (LH), 2 x Persian or Afghan archers (3Bw or Ps), 1 x levies (7Hd) or Afghan spearmen (3Pk) or Persian bow-only cavalry (Cv).

Terrain Type: Dry. **Aggression:** 0. **Enemies** include IV/55a Ottomans.

This list covers the dynasties who ruled Persia as vassals of the Ilkhanid Mongols or emerged in the turmoil following the fall of the Ilkhanate. All Persian cavalry were depicted with "Hollywood Saracen-type" spired helmets with camail, long coats of iron or leather lamellar or mail armour, bow, scimitar and, if a noble or hero, a mace. Some had a long lance and others a conical cane shield, but rarely both. Lancers usually, and others sometimes, rode horses in full lamellar or chequer-patterned quilted silk bards. Only Karts can use Afghans.

References: *Armies of the Middle Ages Vol 2* I. Heath, *Persian Paintings* B. Gray *Children of the Book* P. Carter (novel).

Conflict 32: Battles of the Teutonic Knights.

The most famous battle involving the Teutonic Knights was the Battle of Lake Peipus in 1242 between a Russian Army from the Republic of Novgorod led by Alexander Nevsky and the Livonian branch of the Teutonic Knights. Many of you may have seen the film *Alexander Nevsky,* which includes this battle, and been inspired to recreate this period.

III/79 Early Russian Army 1054-1246 AD: 1 x General (3Kn), 4 x druzhina (3Kn), 2 x Kazaks (LH), 2 x polk (Sp), 1 x smerdy (Sp) or woodsmen (3Ax) or German knights (3Kn/4Bd), 1 x archers (Ps or 3Bw), 1 x ill-armed smerdy (7Hd) or archers (Ps).

Terrain Type: Forest. **Aggression:** 0. **Enemies** include IV/30 Teutonic Knights and IV/35 Mongols.

The Russian list covers the period from the break-up of the Kievan Rus state until the Mongol conquest of Russia. Druzhina were the prince's or boyars' personal troops, in helmet and thigh-length mail or lamellar hauberk, with kite-shaped or small round shield, light lance and sword or mace-and-chain, mounted on unarmoured horses. They were used as a reserve striking force of charging lancers; with horse archers deployed either on their flanks, or in front to provoke enemy to commit prematurely. Kazaks or svoi pogyane "our own pagans" were former nomads (mostly Pecheneg) now settled within the borders and fighting as horse archers, but in scale, mail, lamellar, leather or textile corslets. Infantry formed behind or on the wings. Polk were town militia (mostly armoured spearmen) and Smerdy were peasants of woodland villages, in unbleached linen or wool.

IV/30 Teutonic Order army 1201-1525 AD: 1 x General (3Kn or 6Kn), 1 x ritterbruder (3Kn or 6Kn), 1 x knechte with crossbow (Cv), 3 x crusaders or adventurers (3Kn), 1 x crusaders or adventurers (3Kn) or "Old Prussians" (3Wb), 1 x local turkopolen (LH), 1 x spearmen (Sp), 2 x crossbowmen (4Cb), 1 x Prussian or Livonian levy foot (3Ax or 7Hd).

Terrain Type: Arable. **Aggression:** 4. **Enemies** include IV/35 Mongols & III/79 Russians.

The Teutonic list covers the Teutonic Orders in the Baltic, first the Livonian "Knights of the Sword" founded by the Bishop of Riga from 1200, then from 1226 the Teutonic Knights. It ends with the secularization of the Duchy of Prussia in 1525. Armies usually included 1 or 2 "spitz" wedges with the best armoured knights in front Note that ritterbruder "brother knights" were fully armoured men with heavy lances riding destriers similar to western knights, but knechte were not.

Squabbles between Russians and Teutonic Knights had to be abandoned when the Mongols arrived and attacked them both.

IV/35 Mongol Conquest army 1206-1266 AD: 1 x General (Cv), 2 x Mongol armoured cavalry (Cv) or horse archers (LH), 5 x Mongol horse archers (LH), 1 x Mongol horse archers (LH) or rope-pull stone throwers (Art), 3 x Uighur, Khitan, Khwarizmian or Chinese cavalry (Cv) or Uighur, Cuman, Kipchak, Turkoman or Mongol horse archers (LH).

Terrain Type: Steppe. **Aggression:** 4. **Enemies** include IV/30 Teutonic Knights and III/79 Russians.

The Mongol list covers all Mongolian armies based in Central Asia from Temuchin (better known as Genghis Khan) until the foundation of the Yuan and Ilkhanid Mongol dynasties and the breakaway of the Golden Horde. They differed from previous steppe empires in combining an ideology and discipline. They believed that as there was only one God in heaven, there should be only one ruler on earth; which they attempted to achieve by conquering everyone they met. In 1236, they returned to Europe, conquering the Volga Bulgars in 1237, the Alans in 1239, and Southern Russia in 1238 and 1240, then split in 1241-2 to inflict crushing defeats on the Poles and Teutonics in the north and on the Hungarians in the south, before withdrawing east to choose a new khan. They were organized on a decimal basis up to the touman of 10,000. Military service was due from all fit men from 20 to 61. Western sources say 60-90% of fighters were unarmoured horse archers dressed in blue and brown in summer or furs in winter. These enveloped enemy flanks and prepared the advance of a reserve line of heavy cavalry in mostly boiled leather armour. Conquered peoples provided extra numbers.

References: *Armies of Feudal Europe* I. Heath, *Armies of the Middle Ages Vol 2* I. Heath, *The Teutonic Knights* W. Urban *The Northern Crusades* E. Christiansen, *Armies and Enemies of the Crusades* I. Heath, *The Perilous Frontier* T.J. Barfield, *Defending Heaven* J. Waterson, *The History of the Mongol Conquests* J.J. Saunders, *Until The Sun Falls* C. Holland (novel), *The Year of the Horsetails* R.F. Tapsell (novel).

Conflict 33: The Condottieri in Italy.

Condottieri were capable mercenary leaders hired by a state to provide an army on short or (especially where rulers mistrusted political rivals) long term contracts. Their disciplined men-at-arms "elmetti" could be supported by city militias and sometimes local gentry.

IV/61 Italian Condotta Army 1320 AD - 1515 AD: 1 x General (3Kn), 4 x elmetti (3Kn), 1 x mounted crossbowmen or Hungarian horse archers or Albanian stradiots (LH), 2 x militia crossbowmen (4/8Cb or Ps), 2 x militia (Sp or 4Pk), 1 x Aragonese targeteers (4Ax) or sword-and-buckler men (3Bd) or armed peasants (7Hd), 1 x feudal elmetti (3Kn) or English archers (4Lb) or bombards (Art).

Terrain Type: Littoral if Venice or Genoa, Arable if not. **Aggression:** 1. **Enemies** include IV/5c Sicilians, IV/61 each other, IV/69 Albanians & IV/74 Free Company or Armagnacs

This list covers the armies of Italian city states (primarily Milan, Florence, Pisa, Padua, Naples, Siena, Venice and Genoa) and of the Pope, from the rise of the mercenary companies until the mass use of arquebusiers

IV/5c Sicilian Army 1282-1442AD: 1 x General (3Kn), 3 x knights (3Kn), 1 x Aragonese cavalry (Cv), 1 x Aragonese crossbowmen mixed with shield-men (4Cb), 5 x Catalans (3/4Ax), 1 x Italian communal crossbowmen (8Cb).

Terrain Type: Littoral. **Aggression:** 3. **Enemies** include IV/61 Italian Condottieri.

This list covers Sicily from the "Sicilian Vespers" revolt of 1282 that called in Pere III of Aragon. The revolt ended in 1302 with him as King of Sicily and Charles and his successors ruling in Italy as Kings of Naples. In 1409 Sicily became part of the Kingdom of Aragon.

IV/69 Albanian Army 1345-1430: 1 x General (Cv or LH), 4 x stradiots (LH), 4 x archers (Ps), 1 x archers (3Cb/Ps), 1 x javelinmen (3Ax), 1 x halberdiers (4Bd) or peasants (5Hd) or mercenary men-at-arms (3Kn).

Terrain Type: Hilly. **Aggression:** 1.**Enemies** include IV/61 Italian Condottieri.

After rebelling from Serbia in 1345, Albania fought successfully against the Angevins of Naples and the Venetians before falling to the

Ottomans in 1430. Stradiots are unarmoured Light Horse using a double-ended light lance and light shield.

IV/74 Free Company or Armagnac Armies 1357-1410: 1 x General (3Kn/4Bd), 3 x French or English men-at-arms (3Kn/4Bd), 2 x German or Spanish men-at-arms (3Kn), 3 x English archers (4Lb), 2 x French brigans (3Bd) or English archers (Mtd-4Lb), 1 x crossbowmen (4Cb) or Hungarian horse archers (LH) or Breton javelinmen (Ps).

Terrain Type: Arable. **Aggression:** 4. **Enemies** include IV/61 Italian Condottieri.

This list covers free companies left unemployed by the truce of Bordeaux, the Treaty of Bretigny and later the truce of Tours. It represents army-sized accumulations assembling for major looting expeditions. Many returned to national service when war resumed, but others moved to Italy; including the English "White Company" under Hawkwood and the German "Company of the Star" under Sterz.

References: *Armies of Feudal Europe* I. Heath, *Armies of the Middle Ages* Vol 1 & (for Venice) Vol 2 I. Heath, *Mercenaries and their Masters* M. Mallett, *History of the Art of War in the 16th Century* C. Oman, *Hawkwood in Paris* H. Cole (novel), *Hawkwood and the Towers of Pisa* H. Cole (novel).

Conflict 34: Hundred Years War in France

The "Hundred Years" War lasted, off and on, from 1337 to 1453. When Charles IV of France died, his closest relative was Edward III, king of England, his sister's son. However the French used Salic Law, which prohibits inheritance through the female line.

IV/62b English Army 1334-1414 AD: 1 x General (3Kn/4Bd), 2 x English men-at-arms (4Bd), 1 x archers (4Lb/Mtd-4Lb), 5 x archers (4Lb), 1 x Gascon, Hainaulter or Brabanter men-at-arms (3Kn/4Bd), 1 x Gascon brigans (Sp) or Welsh "knifemen" (3Pk), 1 x Welsh archers (3/4Lb) or Gascon crossbowmen (4Cb).

Terrain Type: Arable. **Aggression**: 3. **Enemies** include IV/64a, IV/64b & IV/64c French

----

IV/62c English Army 1415-1422 AD: 1 x General (3Kn/4Bd), 2 x men-at-arms (3Kn/4Bd), 8 x archers (4Lb), 1 x archers (4Lb) or False-French town militia (4Bd or 4Cb or 7Hd).

Terrain Type: Arable. **Aggression:** 3. **Enemies** include IV/64c French

----

IV/62d English Army 1423-1455 AD: 1 x General (3Kn/4Bd), 1 x men-at-arms (3Kn/4Bd), 8 x archers (4Lb), 1 x billmen (4Bd), 1 x archers (4Lb/Mtd-4Lb) or bombards (Art).

Terrain Type: Arable. **Aggression**: 3. **Enemies** include IV/64c French

These lists cover English armies campaigning in France at Crecy in 1346, Poitiers in 1356, Agincourt in 1415, Verneuil in 1424, Formigny in 1450 and Castilion in 1453. Men-at-arms comprised nobles, bannerets, knights, esquires and gentlemen, the proportion of knights steadily dropping with time. Most of them fought on foot with sword or poleaxe. The bulk of the infantry were longbowmen with bow, sword, dagger, sallet and jack. They are classed as mounted infantry if they retained their horses to change position during the battle. The proportion of longbowmen to men-at-arms increased during the period; and towards its end the latter were supplemented with billmen armed with pole-arms.

IV/64a Medieval French Army 1330-1346 AD: 1 x General (3Kn), 5 x men-at-arms (3Kn), 1 x archers (3Bw) or Spanish crossbowmen (Ps), 2 x Genoese crossbowmen (4Cb) or French crossbowmen (3Cb), 2 x communal militia (Sp), 1 x brigans (3Bd) or bidet or Breton javelinmen (Ps) or peasant levy (7Hd).

Terrain Type: Arable. **Aggression:** 1. **Enemies** include IV/62b English

----

IV/64b Medieval French Army 1347-1400 AD: 1 x General (3Kn/4Bd), 2 x men-at-arms (3Kn/4Bd), 3 x pavisiers (Sp), 2 x crossbowmen (4Cb), 3 x noble knights (3Kn/4Bd) or Jacquerie (5Hd), 1 x bidet or Breton javelinmen (Ps) or peasant levy (7Hd).

Terrain Type: Arable. **Aggression**: 1. **Enemies** include IV/62b English & IV/64b each other.

IV/64c Medieval French Army 1401-1445 AD: 1 x General (3Kn/4Bd), 1 x rich nobles on barded horses (3Kn), 4 x men-at-arms (3Kn/4Bd), 2 x archers (3Bw) or pavisiers (Sp), 1 x crossbowmen (4Cb), 1 x voulgiers (4Bd) or Scots men-at-arms (3Kn/4Bd), 1 x detached "gross varlets" (Cv) or bombards (Art) or Scots archers (4Bw), 1 x bidet or Breton javelinmen (Ps) or peasant levy (7Hd).

Terrain Type: Arable. **Aggression**: 1. **Enemies** include IV/62b, IV/62c & IV/62d English & IV/64c each other.

The French lists cover armies throughout this period. Scots contingents in France were all men-at-arms and archers, not pikemen. Brigans and communal militia came to replace their mixed pole-arms with spear and rectangular pavise. These fought as spearmen, but crossbowmen often carried smaller pavises. Voulgiers discarded the pavise, but were almost as well-armoured as men-at-arms and fought with short two-handed thrusting staff-weapons such as the voulge or langue de boeuf. Jacquerie were revolting peasants.

References: *Armies of the Middle Ages Vol 1* I. Heath, *The Great Warbow* M. Strickland & R. Hardy, *An Alternative History of Britain: The Hundred Years War* T. Venning, *The English Achilles* H. Talbot, *Operation Shepherdess* A. Guerin & J.P. White, *Sir Nigel* A. Conan Doyle (novel), *The White Company* A. Conan Doyle (novel), *A Bloody Field by Shrewsbury* E. Pargeter (Novel), *Azincourt* B. Cornwell (novel), *The Ill-Made Knight* C. Cameron (novel).

Conflict 35: Wars of the Roses.

This civil war between York and Lancaster is often considered to have started during the reign of Henry VI, but it could be argued that the trouble started under Richard II. Richard was forced to abdicate when, having banished his cousin Henry, he confiscated Henry's inheritance. Henry raised an army and invaded England "to claim his inheritance" but it became clear to him that he and his followers could not safely stop there but must claim the crown as well. If this were the starting point, then the Battle of Shrewsbury in 1403 was the first battle in the Wars of the Roses. However there was a long period when the English, under Henry V, were more interested in taking part in the Hundred Year's War against France.

In England, the principle of primogeniture was used to decide who was the rightful king. On Edward's death, Richard II son of Edward's eldest son the Black Prince became king. Edward's second son Lionel Duke of Clarence was next in line, but by the time Richard abdicated, Lionel was dead leaving only a young daughter, and so the crown passed to Henry IV son of Edward's third son John of Gaunt. Later the descendants of Lionel and Edward's fourth son Edmund Duke of York married and combined their claims.

Henry VI was an incompetent king and so the matter was decided on the battlefield. In the first battle, Richard Duke of York and his son Edmund were killed and their claim passed to Richard's son Edward, later crowned as Edward IV. After Henry's death, Edward IV brought several years of peace until he too died, leaving sons too young to rule without a regency. Horrified by the thought of another regency, Parliament was relieved to find that the princes were technically illegitimate so Richard III was offered the crown and became king.

IV/83a Wars of the Roses Armies 1455-1485 AD or Tudor Army 1486-1515 AD: 1 x General (4Bd or 3Kn), 1 x currours (Cv) or border staves (LH) or unreliable levies (7Hd), 4 x stiffened billmen (4Bd), 4 x archers (4Lb), 1 x guns (Art), 1 x Welsh (3Pk) or Irish (3Ax) or men-at-arms (4Bd/3Kn) or mercenary handgunners (Ps).

Terrain Type: Arable. **Aggression**: 1. **Enemies** include IV/83a each other & IV/83b Henry Tudor

Lightly-armoured billmen stiffened by dismounted men-at-arms in full plate were now as important as archers. Armies initially formed with a centre and two wings, all dismounted; but later as a vaward of the best troops, a main body with most of the rest, a rearward of the least reliable and sometimes an elite mounted reserve.

IV/83b Rebel Army of Henry Tudor 1485 AD: 1 x General if Henry mounted but avoiding contact (CP) or if Oxford on foot (4Bd), 1 x exiled noble men-at-arms (4Bd), 4 x French pikemen (4Pk) or French voulgiers (4Bd), 3 x French voulgiers (4Bd) or stiffened English or Welsh billmen (4Bd), 2 x Welsh or English archers (4Lb), 1 x guns (Art) or mercenary crossbowmen or handgunners (Ps).

Terrain Type: Arable. **Aggression**: 1. **Enemy**: IV/83a Richard III.

Two years later in 1485, the Lancastrian heir Henry Tudor (descended from John of Gaunt's illegitimate son and Henry V's widow and actually with a much better claim to the French crown than the English) invaded with the support of the French king and won the Battle of Bosworth where Richard was killed.

IV/83c Rebel Army of Lambert Simnel 1487 AD: 1 x General (4Bd), 1 x billmen (4Bd), 2 x archers (4Lb), 2 x mercenary German and Swiss pikemen (4Pk), 1 x Irish galloglaich (4Bd), 3 x Irish kerns (3Ax), 1 x Irish archers (Ps), 1 x mercenary crossbows or handgunners (Ps).

Terrain Type: Arable. **Aggression: 1. Enemy**: IV/83a Henry VII.

This was nearly the end of the story. By the time Henry Tudor was established on the throne, the "Princes in the Tower" had vanished although rumours abounded that the younger Prince, Richard Duke of York, had escaped. First Lambert Simnel and later Perkin Warbeck arrived at the head of an invading army and claimed to be Richard Duke of York. Both were defeated by the Royal armies and the Tudor succession was now secure.

References: *Armies of the Middle Ages Vol 1* I. Heath, *The Wars of the Roses* A. Goodman, *The Battle of Towton* A.W. Boardman, *Tewkesbury* S. Goodchild, *Richard III and the Bosworth Campaign* P. Hammond, *Lambert Simnel and the Battle of Stoke* M. Bennett, *Army Royal* C.G Cruikshank, *The Military Campaigns of the Wars of the Roses* P.A Haigh.*An Alternative History of Britain: The Wars of the Roses* T. Venning, *The Last Days of Richard III* John Ashdown-Hill, *The Traitors of Bosworth* R. Farrington (novel); *Sun of York* R. Welch (novel), and for a competent dispelling of myth detailing all sources *The Mystery of the Princes* A. Williamson.

Conflict 36: South Seas and Maori.

When we visited New Zealand in 1990 and stayed in Christchurch for the Wargames Convention, I also took the opportunity to visit the Te Maori exhibition in the local museum. Wandering round the exhibits, at first it seemed very strange and exotic and then, it began to feel hauntingly familiar until finally the penny dropped. The Maori were the Vikings of the southern hemisphere. They had the same seafaring skills, the same warrior society, the same strong family ties and the same concept of blood-feud to avenge the death of a family member. Vikings I understand – they are part of my own heritage – and the similarity puts me in sympathy with the Maori.

Before the arrival of the Europeans (pakeha), the Maori in New Zealand fought among themselves. Warfare was their main sport (rugby came later) and was undertaken with great enthusiasm. They used war-canoes to raid other coastal settlements and often built pas (BUAs) so that their opponents could try to capture them. The actual villages, where their families lived and grew food, were excluded from the battle. You may need the stratagems in DBMM to reproduce their full genius in warfare but much can be done in DBA. However the games will need three participants, the two players controlling the armies and an umpire to set the scene and decide on the success of the players.

In a face-to-face battle, two armies of blades lining up and slogging it out do not lead to very interesting battles. However the modelling opportunities for creating the New Zealand scenery, building pas and creating war-canoes in which to visit neighbouring tribes allow scope for great inventiveness. Battles for these armies should be set pieces, just as they were historically, with one side building a pa and issuing a challenge and the other arriving by boat and attempting to capture it.

IV/12e Maori army before 1785 AD: : 1 x General (3Bd), 11 x warriors (3Bd).

Terrain Type: Littoral. **Aggression:** 2. **Enemies:** IV/12e each other.

Maori wore an apron or kilt and broad belt of flax, chiefs adding a dog skin or dark feather cape, tattooed faces and often thighs in dense linear patterns and fought with two-handed weapons such as the taiaha (a hardwood sword with a spear point and feather distracter at the butt end, making it suitable for "bayonet and butt stroke" type fencing), with a shorter whalebone or wooden patu or greenstone mere tucked in the back of the belt.

The Maori were found in New Zealand. Elsewhere in the South Seas we find the other armies who fought each other but are not known to have interacted with the Maori.

IV/12a Fijian, Samoan or Tongan Armies before 1785 A: 1 x General (3Bd), 9 x warriors (3Wb), 2 x slingers or archers (Ps).

Terrain Type: Littoral. **Aggression**: 1. **Enemies:** IV/12a each other, IV/12b other Melanesians, IV/12c other Polynesians and IV/12d Hawaiians.

Fijians, Tongans and Samoans charged fiercely with short two-handed clubs behind a hail of spears and throwing clubs.

IV/12b other Melanesian army before 1785 AD: : 1 x General (3Bd or 4Ax), 9 x warriors (3Ax/3Pk), 2 x slingers or archers (Ps).

Terrain Type: Littoral. **Aggression:** 1. **Enemies:** IV/12a Fijians, Samoans or Tongans, IV/12b each other, IV/12c other Polynesians and IV/12d Hawaiians.

Other Melanesians had long spears, clubs and sometimes small shields, while Polynesians typically fought individual duels with clubs. Coconut fibre armour was sometimes used.

IV/12c other Polynesian army before 1785 AD: : 1 x General (3Bd), 9 x warriors (3Bd), 2 x slingers (Ps).

Terrain Type: Littoral. **Aggression:** 1. **Enemies**: IV/12a Fijians, Samoans or Tongans, IV/12b other Melanisians, IV/12c each other and IV/12d Hawaiians.

IV/12d Hawaiian Army before 1785 AD: 1 x General (4Pk), 1 x alapa and pii pii guard pikemen (4Pk), 2 x papa-kaua pikemen (4Pk) or warriors (3Bd), 5 x warriors (3Bd), 2 x huna-lewa skirmishing javelinmen (Ps), 1 x maka'ainana levies (7Hd).

Terrain Type: Littoral. **Aggression:** 1. **Enemies:** IV/12a Fijians, Samoans or Tongans, IV/12b other Melanisians, IV/12c other Polynesians and IV/12d each other.

In Hawaii, chiefs wore crested helmets and patterned red and yellow feather cloaks and their army had a core of warriors with 15 foot pikes expected to fight to the last man.

References: *Slingshot* 203, *Ancient Hawaii* H. Kane.

Conflict 37: Cortez in America

These conflicts are the earliest interaction between the Europeans and the tribes of Southern America.

IV/19c Spanish & Tlaxcalan army 1518-1521 AD: 1 x Spanish General (3Kn), 1 x Spanish sword-and-buckler men (4Bd), 1 x Spanish crossbowmen and arquebusiers (4Cb), 1 x cannon (Art), 2 x suit-wearers (3Bd or 4Bw), 1 x archers and shield bearers (4Bw), 4 x archers (3/4Bw), 1 x archers (Ps).

Terrain Type: Hilly. **Aggression:** 4. **Enemy** IV/63 Aztec.

Cholula and Tlaxcala, which often allied against the Aztecs. The Tlaxcalans provided most of Cortez' "Spanish" army from 1518. The Spanish thought they maneuvered "marvelously well". They liked to envelope an enemy army's flanks with massed archers before assaulting its centre. The "suit-wearers" (Bd) were military orders such as Eagle, Jaguar and especially Coyote "knights", dressed in appropriate costumes and armed with maquahuitl and shield. Archers had textile armour and side arms and were usually in separate units, but sometimes stiffened with them and protected by their shields. White cotton was not widely available and replaced by dingy maguey or hemp, or for rich men, a mixture.

IV/63 Aztec army: 1 x General (3Bd), 2 x military orders (3Bd), 6 x clan warriors (all 5Hd or all 3Ax), 1 x Ontontin or Cuachic shock troops (3Wb), 2 x slingers or archers (Ps).

Terrain Type: Arable. **Aggression:** 3. Enemies include IV/19a Tarascan & Toltec, IV/19b Chinatec, IV/19c Cortez & his allies and IV/63 each other.

"Aztec" is the most usual name for a people also called "Tenocha" and "Colhua Mexica". They originated as a Chichimec tribe that immigrated into Mexico from the north, absorbed culture from the Toltecs, Mixtecs and Zapotecs and founded the lake island city of Tenochtitlan in 1325. In 1428, this federated with the two nearby lake side cities of Texcoco and Tlacopan to form a unitary Aztec state. This expanded aggressively under Motecuhzoma I, but was conquered by Cortez' Spaniards and his Tlaxcalan allies 1519-1521.

Warriors were organized in numerical units, often distinguished by dress and maintaining loose formation on the march and in battle. The army's main strength lay in its huge numbers, dense showers of missiles (usually javelins thrown by atlatl) and a terrifying cacophony of hideous yells, whistles, conches and drums, but order was quickly lost when group standard-bearers fell, disrupting the decentralized command chain. The primary weapon was the maquahuitl wooden sword edged with razor-sharp obsidian volcanic glass. Military orders are jaguar and a few eagle knights, wearing distinctive suits depicting those creatures. Macehualtin "clan warriors" wore white cotton, sometimes as quilted armour. The option chosen to represent them depends on whether you think rushing about should be emphasized or taking prisoners, but 5Hd produces excellent realistic historical games enjoyed by Aztec players and severely challenges opponents. Macehualtin who took 5 or more prisoners became Ontontin or Cuachic "shorn ones" or "those that hurl themselves to death".

IV/19a Tarascan or Toltec-Chichimec Army: 1 x General (4Bw/3Bd/4Bd), 2 x suit-wearers (3/4Bd), 3 x archers and shield bearers (4Bw), 4 x archers (3Bw), 1 x archers (3Bw) or Otomi mercenaries (3Wb), 1 x archers (Ps).

Terrain Type: Hilly. **Aggression:** 1. **Enemies** IV/19a each other, IV/19b Chinatec and IV/63 Aztec.

IV/19b Chinantec army: 1 x General (4Bw), 1 x nobles (4Bw), 6 x commoners (3Pk), 4 x archers (Ps).

Terrain Type: Hilly. **Aggression**: 1. **Enemies** include IV/19a Tarascan & Toltec or IV/63 Aztec.

The Tarascans and Toltec-Chichimec of Mexico both fought in a similar manner emphasizing the bow, although separated geographically by the Aztecs. The Tarascans (meaning "distant relatives", a mistaken Spanish name for people who actually called themselves "Purempecha") lived west of the Aztecs and fought them to an expensive standoff. To the east of the Aztecs were a number of Toltec-Chichimec city states, of which the most important were Huexotzingo. The Chinantec lived in the mountainous south. Their upper classes fought with bows and hand weapons, while the commoners used "long poles like lances" tipped with long stone cutting edges and leather or fibre shields. They were described as "marching two-by-two" with an archer between each pair of spearmen.

References: *Armies of the 16th Century Vol 2* I. Heath, *Aztec Warfare* R. Hassig, *The True History of the Conquest of New Spain* B. Diaz (an eye-witness account), *Aztec* G. Jennings (novel).

Conflict 38: The Samurai in Japan.

The Samurai list covers Japanese armies from the aftermath of the Mongol invasions until the introduction of European firearms and drilled foot. They mostly fought each other.

IV/59a Samurai Army 1300-1464 AD: 1 x General (6Cv/Cv or 3Bd), 1 x mounted samurai and followers (6Cv/Cv), 4 x samurai (3Bd), 1 x nobushi (4Bw), 1 x ashigaru, follower or Sohei archers (3Bw), 4 x followers mostly with naginata (3Ax) or Sohei (3Bd).

Terrain Type: Hilly. **Aggression:** 0. **Enemies** include IV/59a.

Samurai increasingly fought on foot with the katana sword or the glaive-like naginata. Most wore haramaki armour (lighter than the cumbersome oyoroi of earlier times) but later increasingly added arm and thigh armour. Others fought as nobushi foot archers. The first ashigaru "light-feet" commoner infantry were foot archers, but the Onin War 1467-1477 introduced large numbers of fierce but lightly armoured ashigaru armed instead with the 3-4m (10-12') long yari spear, who later in the 16th century were to evolve into drilled infantry. Those samurai that still fought mounted continued to use bow and "tachi" sword instead of yari and to be closely followed by retainers mostly armed with naginata. They are best represented as 6Cv with the foot in the back row. The naginata-wielding Sohei monks were as turbulent as before but less impetuous. Ikko Ikki were a mass revolutionary movement based not among the peasantry but among artisans from the "temple towns" around Honganji temples. Samurai opposing them were sometimes assisted by town militia that central government thought almost equally seditious. Generals often now directed their armies seated in the rear protected by bodyguards on foot and are then treated as CP.

IV/59b Samurai Army 1465-1542 AD: 1 x General (6Cv/Cv) or if seated on chair (CP), 1 x mounted samurai and followers (6Cv/Cv), 3 x samurai (4Bd), 1 x nobushi (4Bw), 2 x ashigaru with yari (3Pk), 4 x all ashigaru (3Pk) or all Ikko Ikki (5Hd) or all town militia (7Hd) or all Sohei (3Bd).

Terrain Type: Hilly. **Aggression:** 0. **Enemies** include IV/59b.

References: *Weapons and Fighting Techniques of the Samurai Warrior 1200-1877 AD* T. D. Conlan, *Samurai* Mitsuo Kure, *Battles of the Samurai* S. Turnbull, *Soldiers of the Dragon* C. Peers, *The Perilous Frontier* T.J. Barfield, *Defending Heaven* J. Waterson.

Chapter Seven: What Next?

Having bought this book, produced a couple of armies and tried out a few games, the question of what to do next will arise. You may be lucky enough to have a large friendly wargames club nearby in which case you will be able to join it and will gain much in both knowledge and companionship. While I do know how to contact specific clubs at the present time, that information soon becomes out-of-date. The best advice I can give you is to search online or on social media such as *Facebook* using the term "wargames" and the name of your country, district or town. You may also wish to contact the online groups such as groups.yahoo.cpm/group/*DBA* or the Fanaticus group.

However there are many areas in which there are no existing clubs nearby and you will have to manage by yourself. Get a few friends interested and start your own club. It's not difficult and can be very rewarding. The smallest clubs I know have run for many months with just three members.

Joining the Society of Ancients is an excellent way to learn about wargames and military history in the pre-gunpowder period. Its bi-monthly journal SLINGSHOT balances research of a very high standard with more specifically wargaming content. Contact: *www.soa.org.uk* for more details of meetings and membership.

I would also recommend attending the occasional Wargames Convention. These may be found worldwide. Again you can search online – I searched for "wargames conventions" and found the site gameconventionscentral.com which listed such meetings worldwide and organised by area. Once you attend such a meeting, you will find many other wargamers who can give you information about clubs in your area. The dealers area will allow you to contact local hobby shops who will also have information about their customers and this will help to meet others in your area. The convention website may have details about the club or clubs organising it – for example the website for Genghis Con in Denver also gives a link to *www.denvergamers.org* and this allows a newcomer in the Denver area to contact the club without waiting for the next Genghis Con. The large conventions on the east coast of the USA are *Cold Wars*, *Historicon* and *Fall In* and these are described on the HMGS website – these conventions are huge and draw crowds from a large area including a few participants from the UK. I have attended in the past, but am now too old to travel that far.

In the UK there are many annual events and most of them are advertised in publications such as "Slingshot" or online. They are also included in the gameconventionscentral.com website. There are more general sites, such as that for the BHGS, which have a list of local clubs. However you may be more successful if you try to find the club directly – for example if you type "Shrewsbury Wargames" you will find the link for *www.swgs.org.uk* and this has the information you need to contact this club.

If you live in the UK, you may wish to join Wargame Developments. This is not for the faint-hearted, but if you don't suffer from delicate susceptibilities then attending "COW" their annual weekend *Conference of Wargamers* is an enjoyable and memorable experience. It's one of the highlights of my year. Contact: *www.wargamedevelopments.org* for information about membership of WD, COW and their journal the Nugget.

You may wish to buy other books on the subject and a few are mentioned here.

De Bellis Antiquitatis 3.0. Since this book is an introduction to the *DBA* rules, some of you may outgrow it and wish to buy the full DBA rules. You may feel cheated and indignant at the suggestion that you need to buy a second book but that's only necessary if you want to use the extra information. If all you wish to do is play DBA games, this book has all you need and many of you will spend years playing ancient wargames without needing anything else. The final chapter of this book contains about 50 armies – the full DBA rules have about ten times that number. It would not be possible to include the whole set of army lists in a book of this size and so if you want the extra selection of armies you will need access to the full DBA – either borrowing a copy from a friend or buying your own.

De Bellis Magistrorum Militum (*DBMM*) and its Army Lists. DBA is a fast and simple set of rules which represents an entire army in 12 elements. This inevitably loses some of the detail of ancient warfare. Some of you may wish to zoom in and study the battles in more detail. *DBMM* does this. It is a more detailed set of rules, more figures on the table and more opportunities for using the clever stratagems employed by the ancient generals. You can include flank marches and the effects of weather. If you want to spend time on all these details you will find *DBMM* more to your taste. However the greater detail does cause greater complexity and games take longer – if you commonly take half-an-hour for a *DBA* game, you will probably take two or three hours to fight the same game under *DBMM*.

The website for WRG Ltd _www.wargamesresearchgroup.net_ contains details of all current WRG publications.

John Curry's _The History of Wargaming Project_ reprints an increasing number of normally inaccessible early wargames rules and books, including (with permission) several out-of-print WRG titles. He has also published a collection of early versions of _DBA_ (under the title _DBA 2.2_) starting with the two-page _DBSA_ in 1989 then _DBA_ version 1 published in 1990 and _DBA_ version 2.2 published in 2004. Information on these and all his many other publications may be seen on his website _www.wargaming.co_ which is continually updated as the number of publications increases. For the really isolated, he has reprinted some books on Solo Wargaming.

I have described my methods for producing and painting armies and these will provide a good introduction. For more information, you may wish to use other books, such as "The Wargaming Compendium" by Henry Hyde, which will give different methods to try out.

Whichever of these you choose, I hope you will get as much enjoyment from your wargaming as I have done.

Sue Laflin Barker. November 2014.

INDEX OF ARMY LISTS

INDEX OF ARMY LISTS
IN CHRONOLOGICAL ORDER